# Martin D. Caldwell

## The Divine Code
## Aeons and Esoteric Christianity

**Original Title:** The Divine Code: Aeons and Esoteric Christianity

**Copyright © 2024, published by Luiz Antonio dos Santos ME.** This book is a non-fiction work that explores the principles and mystical insights of Esoteric Christianity, particularly focusing on the role of the Aeons in the spiritual cosmology. Through a comprehensive approach, the author presents practical tools for spiritual awakening, personal transformation, and the attainment of higher knowledge and divine connection.

**1st Edition**

**Production Team**

**Author:** Martin D. Caldwell
**Editor:** Luiz Santos
**Cover:** Studios Booklas / Ethan Carter
**Consultant:** Sophia Mendes
**Researchers:** Daniel K. Hughes / Maria Celeste / Jonathan Reyes
**Layout Designer:** Marcus R. Allen

**Publication and Identification**

The Divine Code: Aeons and Esoteric Christianity
Booklas, 2024
**Categories:** Esoteric Christianity / Gnosticism / Mysticism
**DDC:** 273.1 (Gnosticism) — **CDU:** 27-1 (Christian heresies and sects - Gnosticism)

All rights reserved to:

**Luiz Antonio dos Santos ME / Booklas**

No part of this book may be reproduced, stored in a retrieval system, or transmitted by any means — electronic, mechanical, photocopy, recording, or otherwise — without the prior written permission of the copyright holder.

# Summary

Sistematic Index ........................................................................... 5
Foreword ....................................................................................... 9
Chapter 1 Perspective Beyond Dogma ..................................... 13
Chapter 2 The Understanding of the Aeons ............................. 20
Chapter 3 The Field of Divine Forces........................................ 28
Chapter 4 Cosmic Intelligences ................................................. 36
Chapter 5 Religious and Philosophical Context ....................... 44
Chapter 6 The Divine Fullness................................................... 52
Chapter 7 Aeonic Hierarchy ...................................................... 59
Chapter 8 The Cosmic Fall ........................................................ 66
Chapter 9 Christ the Savior Aeon ............................................. 74
Chapter 10 The Holy Spirit, the Feminine Aeon ...................... 81
Chapter 11 Creation of the Material World .............................. 88
Chapter 12 Functions of the Aeons............................................ 95
Chapter 13 Aeons and Time....................................................... 102
Chapter 14 Aeonic Variations.................................................... 109
Chapter 15 Criticisms of the Concept........................................ 117
Chapter 16 The Redemptive Mission of Christ ........................ 124
Chapter 17 Christ in the Aeonic Hierarchy.............................. 130
Chapter 18 The Mission of Christ in the Material World ........ 136
Chapter 19 The Gospel of Truth and the Aeon Christ ............. 142
Chapter 20 The Secret Teachings of the Christ Aeon............... 148
Chapter 21 Aeonic Christ and Historical Jesus........................ 154

Chapter 22 Path to Salvific Knowledge ................................... 161
Chapter 23 Return to the Pleroma ............................................ 167
Chapter 24 The Sacrifice of the Aeon Christ ........................... 174
Chapter 25 Harmony and Cooperation in the Divine Realm .... 181
Chapter 26 Personal Spiritual Practice ..................................... 188
Chapter 27 Knowledge of the Aeons ........................................ 194
Chapter 28 Guides on the Spiritual Path .................................. 200
Chapter 29 The Awakening to Divine Reality ......................... 206
Chapter 30 Aeons in Contemporary Spirituality ...................... 212
Chapter 31 The Human Evolution and Esoteric Christianity ... 218
Epilogue ................................................................................... 224

# Sistematic Index

**Chapter 1: Perspective Beyond Dogma** - Introduces the concept of Esoteric Christianity as a path to deeper faith.

**Chapter 2: The Understanding of the Aeons** - Unveils the Aeons, divine emanations that structure reality.

**Chapter 3: The Field of Divine Forces** - Explores the Gnostic view of the universe as a dynamic field of spiritual interactions.

**Chapter 4: Cosmic Intelligences** - Discusses the Aeons as real and active intelligences in the cosmos.

**Chapter 5: Religious and Philosophical Context** - Explores the historical and philosophical roots of the concept of Aeons.

**Chapter 6: The Divine Fullness** - Unveils the Pleroma, the realm of divine fullness and the dwelling place of the Aeons.

**Chapter 7: Aeonic Hierarchy** - Details the hierarchical structure and organization of the Aeons in the Pleroma.

**Chapter 8: The Cosmic Fall** - Narrates the fall of the Aeon Sophia and its implications for the creation of the material world.

**Chapter 9: Christ the Savior Aeon** - Presents the Aeon Christ as a redemptive emanation from the Pleroma.

**Chapter 10: The Holy Spirit, the Feminine Aeon** - Explores the Holy Spirit as a feminine Aeon, a source of life and inspiration.

**Chapter 11: Creation of the Material World** - Discusses the Gnostic view of the creation of the material world by the Demiurge.

**Chapter 12: Functions of the Aeons** - Details the various functions of the Aeons, including cosmic organization, human evolution, and redemption.

**Chapter 13: Aeons and Time** - Explores the relationship between the Aeons and time, contrasting Aeonic eternity with human linear time.

**Chapter 14: Aeonic Variations** - Discusses the variations in the understanding and organization of the Aeons in different Gnostic systems.

**Chapter 15: Criticisms of the Concept** - Presents historical criticisms of the concept of Aeons and its modern reinterpretations.

**Chapter 16: The Redemptive Mission of Christ** - Deepens the discussion on the redemptive mission of the Aeon Christ, focusing on its Gnostic interpretation.

**Chapter 17: Christ in the Aeonic Hierarchy** - Analyzes the position and role of Christ within the Aeonic hierarchy.

**Chapter 18: The Mission of Christ in the Material World** - Discusses the purpose and implications of the Aeon Christ's descent into the material world.

**Chapter 19: The Gospel of Truth and the Aeon Christ** - Examines the Gospel of Truth and its presentation of the Aeon Christ as the revealer of the Father.

**Chapter 20: The Secret Teachings of the Christ Aeon** - Explores the secret teachings of the Aeon Christ, particularly in the Gospel of Thomas.

**Chapter 21: Aeonic Christ and Historical Jesus** - Differentiates and integrates the perspectives of the Aeonic Christ and the Historical Jesus.

**Chapter 22: Path to Salvific Knowledge** - Discusses the path to Gnosis and the role of the Aeon Christ in this journey.

**Chapter 23: Return to the Pleroma** - Describes the process of return to the Pleroma, the realm of divine fullness, as the culmination of the spiritual journey.

**Chapter 24: The Sacrifice of the Aeon Christ** - Reinterprets the sacrifice of Christ from the Aeonic perspective, emphasizing his descent into the material world.

**Chapter 25: Harmony and Cooperation in the Divine Realm** - Highlights the harmony and cooperation among the Aeons in the Pleroma and their implications for human redemption.

**Chapter 26: Personal Spiritual Practice** - Offers guidance on personal spiritual practice aimed at connecting with the Aeons.

**Chapter 27: Knowledge of the Aeons** - Deepens the discussion on the knowledge of the Aeons, emphasizing Gnosis as a direct experience of the divine realm.

**Chapter 28: Guides on the Spiritual Path** - Explores the role of the Aeons as guides and mentors on the spiritual path, offering inspiration, protection, and wisdom.

**Chapter 29: The Awakening to Divine Reality** - Describes the process of awakening to divine reality, driven by the influence of the Aeons and the practice of Gnosis.

**Chapter 30: Aeons in Contemporary Spirituality** - Discusses the relevance of the concept of Aeons for contemporary spirituality and its ability to respond to modern anxieties and yearnings.

**Chapter 31: The Human Evolution and Esoteric Christianity** - Presents an evolutionary vision of humanity from the perspective of esoteric Christianity, highlighting the role of the Aeons in this process.

# Foreword

There is knowledge so ancient and so essential that its mere existence threatens the foundations of the visible world. These are fragments of a primeval truth, whose roots intertwine with the hidden currents of humanity's own spiritual history. Among these immaterial relics, a concept resurfaces—silenced for centuries, hidden by veils of dogmas and forgetfulness—and now, for the first time, revealed with clarity and depth. Allow yourself to awaken to the Aeons, the invisible threads that sustain the multiplicity of the universe, the divine intelligences that precede matter and transcend the linear understanding of time.

What you are about to read is not just a work; it is a key. Each word, each revealed concept, opens a portal to a hidden universe, buried under layers of doctrines, persecutions, and censored narratives. The Aeons—emanations of the supreme divine source—are the living memory of the cosmos, a luminous network that connects each being to the transcendent origin. They are not myths, nor distant symbols. They inhabit the structure of reality and have pulsed, since the beginning, in the core of your forgotten consciousness.

Since the early centuries of the Christian era, bold voices whispered about these cosmic guardians.

Spiritual masters and silent mystics knew them, not as theological abstractions, but as living presences, ordering forces that shape not only the invisible worlds but also human destinies. These masters knew that true knowledge could only be achieved when the individual recognized their own divine spark—a spark whose origin is intertwined with the Aeons themselves.

At the heart of the ancient Gnostic circles, the Aeons were revered as living portals between the divine and the human. They form a golden chain of wisdom and light, a luminous hierarchy that spirals down from the primordial source to the furthest reaches of material creation. Each Aeon carries a sacred name, a unique vibration, and a cosmic function, preserving universal harmony and guiding souls on their journey of return. To understand the Aeons is to unravel the hidden map of the cosmos and the human soul.

However, this wisdom was condemned to silence. With the consolidation of dogmatic Christianity and the strengthening of the institutional Church, everything that offered the individual direct access to the divine became dangerous and heretical. The concept of Aeons was ripped from sacred texts, relegated to the apocrypha, and buried in secret libraries and codices buried in forgotten deserts. The great ecclesiastical councils, by establishing a distant and authoritarian God, denied man the right to remember his sacred lineage and his direct connection with the agents of creation.

This book rescues what time and power have tried to obliterate. Here, you will not find superficial explanations or simplified doctrines. What is presented before your eyes is a revelation—a reconstruction of the integral, mystical, and cosmic knowledge that pulsates in the subtext of rejected gospels, in the echoes of hermetic traditions, and in the whispers preserved by the initiates of ancient wisdom.

Each page is a call to remembrance. By understanding the Aeons, you do not just read about them; you recognize them within yourself. They are not just external forces—they are extensions of your own essence, fragments of the divine intelligence that inhabits your dormant spirit. Each Aeon resonates in your soul like a forgotten memory, a lost note of the original symphony that makes up your true spiritual identity.

You have been conditioned to believe that your faith should be mediated, your connection with the divine filtered by dogmas and external authorities. This lie, sustained for centuries, will dissolve before your eyes as you progress through these pages. Here, each concept is not only explained—it is returned to you. You will understand that your soul is not a subject, but an heir; that your spiritual quest is not a submission, but a recovery of what has always belonged to you: the direct connection with the higher spheres, with the Aeons, and with the divine fullness of which you are an inseparable part.

Allow yourself the transformative experience of remembering. Delve into the forgotten roots of esoteric Christianity, where the sacred is alive and accessible, where symbols are portals, and where mystical experience is the true key to redemption. Open yourself to the discomfort of relearning, of questioning the foundations on which your spirituality was built, and let the memory of the Aeons rebuild your inner path.

What you hold now is not just a book—it is a mirror. As you look through it, you will see not only the hidden universe but also the forgotten face of your own soul. You are a fragment of the primordial light, a living particle of the Pleroma. And the Aeons, these silent masters, extend their luminous hands to guide you back to fullness.

May this reading be not only informative but initiatory. That by crossing the threshold of these pages, you not only learn—but awaken. For the call of the Aeons echoes in every soul that dares to remember. And now, that call is yours.

Luiz Santos Editor

# Chapter 1
# Perspective Beyond Dogma

Esoteric Christianity reveals itself as a profound and transformative dimension of the Christian faith, going beyond conventional and dogmatic interpretations to explore the innermost and symbolic aspects of the Christian tradition. While institutionalized Christianity often emphasizes adherence to established doctrines and ritualistic practices accessible to all believers, esoteric Christianity is directed towards those who seek a more intimate and mystical understanding of the sacred. This path does not intend to deny or contradict traditional faith, but to expand it, offering a vision that transcends the surface of scriptures and religious teachings to reach their deepest essence. Thus, its approach is not based exclusively on dogmatic belief, but on the direct experience of the divine, on the symbolic interpretation of sacred texts, and on spiritual practice aimed at inner awakening. The distinction between exotericism and esotericism in Christianity does not imply a rigid or exclusive division, but reflects different levels of understanding and deepening of faith, enabling those who feel a call to the inner search to find a path of spiritual expansion and enlightenment.

Since the early days of the Christian era, esoteric currents emerged as part of the development of the Christian tradition, manifesting in various forms and influences. Among the early Christians, there were communities that understood Christ's message not only as a moral and ethical teaching but as an invitation to the transformation of consciousness and mystical union with God. Movements such as Christian Gnosticism, Hermetic writings, and monastic mystical traditions were some of the expressions of this search for hidden knowledge and direct spiritual experience. The esoteric approach to Christianity has always been present throughout history, although it has often been marginalized or repressed by religious institutions that feared its emphasis on spiritual autonomy and personal revelation. However, its legacy remains alive, influencing thinkers, mystics, and spiritual seekers who recognize in the Christian faith not only a belief system but a path of inner transformation and divine realization.

Esoteric Christianity is based on the conviction that the scriptures and teachings of Christ contain multiple levels of meaning, which go beyond literal and dogmatic reading. The parables, symbols, and events narrated in the Bible are considered portals to hidden spiritual truths, accessible to those who develop the discernment and inner sensitivity necessary to understand them. The Christian esoteric quest is not limited to intellectual study but involves contemplative practices, meditation, deep prayer, and spiritual disciplines that aid in the elevation of consciousness and direct connection with the divine. By adopting this perspective, esoteric Christianity rescues the mystical tradition of Christianity, offering an approach that emphasizes personal experience and authentic spiritual living. In a world where spirituality is often lost in formalities and superficialities, this tradition invites the seeker to delve into the depths of faith, rediscovering its richness, depth, and transformative potential.

Exotericism, in its broadest sense, refers to knowledge that is public, accessible to all, and intended for the general mass of believers. In the context of Christianity, exotericism manifests itself in common doctrines and practices, in the teachings openly transmitted by religious institutions, and in literal interpretations of sacred scriptures. The emphasis is on adherence to a set of established beliefs, participation in community rituals, and obedience to prescribed moral precepts. Exoteric Christianity, therefore, prioritizes dogmatic faith, doctrinal conformity, and ethical conduct within the limits defined by established religious tradition.

In contrast, esotericism concerns knowledge that is considered hidden, reserved for a restricted circle of initiates or more advanced spiritual seekers. This esoteric knowledge is not necessarily secret in the sense of being forbidden or prohibitive, but rather in the sense that its understanding requires a level of discernment, experience, and inner preparation that not everyone possesses or seeks to develop. In Christianity, esotericism seeks to unravel the symbolic and allegorical meanings of scriptures, explore the mystical dimensions of religious experience, and unveil the mysteries underlying the Christian faith. Esoteric Christianity, therefore, emphasizes personal mystical experience, the inner search for spiritual truth, and the transformation of consciousness through esoteric knowledge and practice.

It is important to emphasize that the distinction between exoteric and esoteric Christianity does not imply a hierarchy of value or an irreconcilable opposition. Both approaches can coexist and even complement each other in an individual's spiritual journey. Exoteric Christianity offers a fundamental structure of beliefs, rituals, and values that can serve as a starting point and community support for many. Esoteric Christianity, on the other hand, offers a path of deepening and internalization for those who feel a call to explore the deeper and more mysterious dimensions of faith.

Esoteric Christianity is not limited to a single denomination or school of thought. Throughout the history of Christianity, various esoteric currents have emerged, manifesting in different forms and expressions. Some of these currents emphasize the Western mystical tradition, seeking connections with Christian Kabbalah, spiritual alchemy, and Hermeticism. Other currents are inspired by Gnostic sources and apocryphal texts, seeking to rescue a more comprehensive and complex vision of Christian cosmology and soteriology. Still other currents focus on the practice of contemplative prayer, meditation, and other spiritual disciplines aimed at cultivating the direct experience of God and mystical union with the divine.

Regardless of their particularities, all forms of esoteric Christianity share some common characteristics. Firstly, all emphasize the importance of personal and direct experience of God, above blind adherence to dogmas or mere observance of external rituals. Esoteric faith is not merely an intellectual belief or a social convention, but a living and transformative search for the divine presence in the innermost being.

Secondly, esoteric Christianity values the symbolic and allegorical interpretation of scriptures. Biblical narratives are not seen only as historical accounts or moral commandments but as vehicles of deeper spiritual teachings, which can be unveiled through intuition, contemplation, and esoteric study. The symbols and metaphors present in the scriptures are considered keys to accessing more subtle layers of meaning and to awakening spiritual understanding.

Thirdly, esoteric Christianity recognizes the existence of a hidden or mysterious dimension in reality, which transcends the material and sensible world. This mysterious dimension is seen as the source of life, consciousness, and spirituality, and as the true home of the human soul. The esoteric quest aims to unveil this mystery and reconnect the human soul with its divine origin.

Fourthly, esoteric Christianity often incorporates specific spiritual practices, such as meditation, contemplative prayer, creative visualization, and other techniques that aid in internalization, expansion of consciousness, and mystical experience. These practices are seen as tools to refine perception, silence the rational mind, and open oneself to intuition and divine inspiration.

In the current context, the study of esoteric Christianity assumes particular relevance. In a world increasingly secularized and materialistic, many people feel a longing for a deeper and more meaningful spirituality, which goes beyond the superficial and dogmatic forms of conventional religion. Esoteric Christianity offers a path to satisfy this longing, providing a richer, more complex, and transformative vision of the Christian faith.

Furthermore, the study of esoteric Christianity can contribute to a broader and more ecumenical dialogue between different spiritual and religious traditions. By exploring the universal principles underlying the various manifestations of Christian esotericism, we can discover points of convergence and mutual understanding with other currents of mystical and esoteric thought, both within and outside of Christianity.

Esoteric Christianity can also play an important role in revitalizing the Christian faith in the face of contemporary challenges. By rescuing the mystical and contemplative dimensions of the Christian tradition, esotericism can offer an answer to the crisis of meaning and the search for spiritual authenticity that mark our time. By emphasizing personal experience and inner transformation, esoteric Christianity can make the Christian faith more relevant, vibrant, and meaningful for individuals and for society as a whole.

Exploring esoteric Christianity is, therefore, embarking on a fascinating and transformative journey towards the heart of the Christian faith. It is opening oneself to a perspective that challenges the boundaries of dogma, that values experience above belief, and that invites us to discover the mysterious and divine dimension that resides in our own interior and in all things. By delving into the depths of esoteric Christianity, we can rediscover the richness and depth of the Christian message in a new and invigorating way, finding a path of spiritual growth, self-knowledge, and union with the divine.

# Chapter 2
# The Understanding of the Aeons

The understanding of the Aeons in the context of esoteric Christianity emerges as a central element in unraveling the complex network of relationships between the primordial divinity, the cosmos, and the human soul. Far from the simplified vision of a single, personal God who acts directly on creation and history, esoteric Christianity describes a multifaceted reality, where the divine unfolds in a sequence of spiritual emanations that structure both the visible universe and the hidden dimensions of existence. These emanations, known as Aeons, form a hierarchical chain of spiritual intelligences that, over successive generations, sustain the cosmic order and preserve the connection between the transcendent source and the lower spheres of creation. Each Aeon expresses a quality or essential attribute of the supreme divinity, such as truth, wisdom, light, and love, functioning as channels through which the divine consciousness permeates and animates all things. The existence and function of these beings are not peripheral speculations or mere theological abstractions; they constitute the very backbone of Gnostic cosmology and the spiritual quest proposed by this tradition, where the ascension of the soul and its reintegration into the divine necessarily pass through the recognition and conscious interaction with these spiritual powers.

Contrary to the conception of a creator God who shapes the world *ex nihilo* by a voluntary and sovereign act, esoteric Christianity describes the manifestation of the universe as a process of internal unfolding of divinity itself. Within this model, the Pleroma—the divine fullness—houses all the Aeons, beings that emerge progressively from the original source, each reflecting a specific aspect of the divine infinite. This process of emanation, far from being arbitrary, obeys an intrinsic order, where each new Aeon arises as a consequence of the dynamic relationship between those that preceded it. This chain of spiritual intelligences forms an uninterrupted current between the ineffable and the manifest, between what transcends all form and what becomes discernible to the senses and the mind. This spiritual hierarchy is not a simple mythological description, but a symbolic map that guides the seeker on the path of spiritual ascension. By understanding and recognizing the presence of the Aeons, the adept begins to see reality not as a field of chaotic or disconnected forces, but as a living web of spiritual intelligences that sustain the universal order and actively participate in the cosmic drama of redemption and the return to primordial unity.

The function of the Aeons is not limited to the preservation of the cosmic order; they are also the guardians of spiritual knowledge and the mediators between humanity and the divine. Each Aeon, as it emanates from the source, carries within it a portion of the primordial Gnosis—the deep and direct knowledge of the true nature of being and reality. This knowledge, however, is obscured by the emergence of the material world, a domain separate from the Pleroma, marked by imperfections and illusions. The Gnostic tradition frequently portrays this distancing as a result of a cosmic flaw, associated with the figure of Sophia, whose unbalanced emanation gives rise to the Demiurge—the imperfect creator of the physical world. Yet, even in this context of separation and forgetfulness, the Aeons remain active, shedding light on the hidden path that leads the soul back to its true home. Throughout apocryphal texts and Gnostic treatises, Christ is often described as a redeeming Aeon, the one who descends to the lower regions not only to teach, but to awaken, within each human being, the dormant memory of his or her spiritual origin. Thus, understanding the Aeons and establishing a conscious link with them represents much more than an intellectual exercise; it is an act of ontological reconnection, a retrieval of the lost thread that unites the soul to the divine. In this process, esoteric cosmology is converted into practical spirituality, where knowing is transforming oneself and remembering is liberating oneself.

The concept of Aeons is widely documented in the Gnostic texts discovered in the Nag Hammadi library and in the Apocryphal Gospels, sources that reveal an alternative vision of early Christianity. These writings not only describe the genealogy of the Aeons and their function in the universal order, but also emphasize the split between the material world and the spiritual world. According to this tradition, the physical universe is not the direct creation of the supreme divinity, but the result of a distancing or fall of one of the Aeons, often identified with Sophia (Wisdom). This cosmic error leads to the emergence of the Demiurge, an imperfect entity that shapes the material world and imposes upon it a veil of ignorance and illusion. From this cosmology, the human condition is seen as a state of spiritual imprisonment, where matter and the limitations imposed by time and space distance the soul from its true origin. Thus, the understanding of the Aeons becomes fundamental to the journey of redemption, for it is these entities that, through the emanation of Christ as a redeeming Aeon, offer humanity the way to transcend the physical world and return to the Pleroma.

The study of the Aeons in esoteric Christianity is not limited to theological speculation, but has direct implications for spirituality and the practice of the inner quest. The revelation of these beings as intermediaries between the human and the divine suggests a model of spiritual ascension based on the awakening of consciousness and the reintegration with the higher principles of existence. Different Gnostic traditions propose various methods to achieve this reintegration, including initiation rituals, contemplative practices, and the symbolic decoding of scriptures. In essence, the knowledge of the Aeons is not only a key to understanding the structure of the cosmos, but a path to personal liberation, where the seeker, by recognizing his or her divine origin, breaks with the shackles of ignorance and reconnects with the spiritual totality. By bringing this perspective to light, esoteric Christianity broadens the understanding of the sacred, offering a path that goes beyond conventional faith and enters the domains of mystical knowledge and inner transformation.

Initially, it is fundamental to define what is meant by the Apocryphal Gospels. The term "apocryphal," derived from the Greek "apokryphos" (hidden, secret), historically designated writings of religious origin whose authenticity or canonicity was questioned by ecclesiastical authorities. In the context of early Christianity, various texts were produced that narrated the life of Jesus, his teachings, and the events related to the apostles, parallel to the canonical Gospels of Matthew, Mark, Luke, and John. These texts, called Apocryphal Gospels, encompass a variety of literary genres and theological perspectives, reflecting the diversity and effervescence of religious thought in the first centuries of the Christian era.

It is important to emphasize that the designation of "apocryphal" does not necessarily imply that these gospels are false, heretical, or devoid of spiritual value. In many cases, the exclusion of these texts from the biblical canon was motivated by complex historical, theological, and political criteria, related to the consolidation of ecclesiastical power and the definition of doctrinal orthodoxy. However, the Apocryphal Gospels preserve traditions and views that, although not incorporated into the official canon, offer valuable insights into the history of early Christianity and the evolution of religious ideas of the time. Among the vast range of apocryphal gospels, some stand out for their relevance to the study of the Aeons, such as the Gospel of Thomas, the Gospel of Philip, the Protoevangelium of James, and the Gospel of Peter.

The discovery of the Nag Hammadi library in 1945 represented a fundamental milestone for the understanding of esoteric Christianity and, in particular, for the study of the Aeons. Nag Hammadi is the name of a locality in Upper Egypt, where a peasant accidentally found a set of ancient codices buried in a clay jar. These codices, written in Coptic, contained a collection of texts of a religious and philosophical nature, dated from the 3rd and 4th centuries AD. The Nag Hammadi library includes a variety of works, encompassing gospels, acts, epistles, apocalypses, and treatises, many of which belong to the Gnostic tradition.

The importance of the Nag Hammadi discovery lies in the fact that these texts offer direct access to a form of early Christianity that had been largely marginalized and obscured by history. Before Nag Hammadi, knowledge about Gnosticism was primarily derived from polemical and fragmentary accounts by orthodox Christian authors, who frequently distorted and caricatured Gnostic ideas in order to refute them. The Nag Hammadi codices, on the other hand, provide the Gnostic texts themselves, allowing scholars and spiritual seekers to access the primary sources and understand Gnosticism in its own terms.

Within the Nag Hammadi library, several texts stand out for their relevance to the study of the Aeons. The Apocryphon of John, for example, presents a detailed Gnostic cosmology, describing the emanation of the Aeons from the divine Monad, the creation of the material cosmos by the imperfect Demiurge, and the role of the Aeons in the redemption of humanity. The Gospel of Truth, another fundamental text from Nag Hammadi, offers a poetic and profound meditation on the Aeon Christ as the revealer of Gnosis and guide for the return to the Pleroma, the divine dwelling of the Aeons. The Tripartite Tractate explores the hierarchy and functions of the Aeons in a systematic way, detailing their relationships and their contributions to the cosmic order. The Gospel of Philip, in turn, presents reflections on the sacraments and Gnostic practices, using a symbolic language rich in references to the Aeons.

When studying the Apocryphal Gospels and the texts of Nag Hammadi, it is crucial to approach these sources with a careful eye and critical discernment. It is important to recognize that these texts reflect a diversity of perspectives and interpretations, and that not all of them present a univocal or coherent view on the Aeons. Some texts emphasize the transcendent and ineffable nature of the Aeons, while others focus on their cosmic and soteriological functions. Some texts describe complex hierarchies of Aeons, while others present simpler lists or focus on specific Aeons.

Despite this diversity, it is possible to identify some recurring themes and ideas in the apocryphal and

Nag Hammadi texts in relation to the Aeons. In general, the Aeons are described as emanations of the Supreme Divinity, cosmic intelligences and organizing forces that participate in the creation and maintenance of the cosmos. They are seen as intermediaries between the transcendent world and the material world, acting as agents of the divine will and mediators of revelation and redemption. Christ, in many Gnostic texts, is identified as a prominent Aeon, sent to the material world to awaken humanity to Gnosis and guide it back to its divine origin.

Therefore, the Apocryphal Gospels and the Nag Hammadi library represent indispensable primary sources for understanding the concept of the Aeons within esoteric Christianity. These texts invite us to explore a broader and deeper view of the Christian faith, which recognizes the existence of a hierarchy of spiritual beings that participate in the organization of the cosmos and the evolution of humanity. By delving into these sources, we can enrich our understanding of Christian cosmology, soteriology, and spirituality, and discover hidden and fascinating dimensions of the Western religious tradition. The journey through the Apocryphal Gospels and Nag Hammadi is an invitation to expand our worldview and rediscover the richness and complexity of the esoteric Christian legacy.

# Chapter 3
# The Field of Divine Forces

Gnostic cosmology reveals the universe as a vast and intricate field of spiritual interactions, where forces of divine nature and manifestations of a lower order coexist in a dynamic tension, shaping both the hidden structure of reality and the human experience in the material world. This vision offers a deeply nuanced understanding of the cosmos, presenting existence not as a linear and ordered creation by a personal and sovereign God, but as the result of a continuous process of spiritual emanations, where each level of reality emerges as an unfolding from a previous principle, progressively further away from the supreme source. This process of emanation, far from being merely a chronological sequence of events, reflects a cosmic architecture in which each layer of existence, from the luminous Pleroma to the dense material world, carries within it traces of the divine essence, albeit veiled by layers of forgetfulness, limitation, and distortion. In this vibrant field of spiritual forces, the Aeons represent active powers, entities that channel specific aspects of the primordial divinity, configuring themselves as living archetypes that sustain the cosmic order, while the Demiurge and his hosts represent forces of closure, imprisonment, and illusion, which crystallize matter and obscure the memory of humanity's true spiritual origin.

The interaction between these forces is not a Manichean conflict of good versus evil in its simplistic conception, but a structural tension that permeates the totality of existence and is directly reflected in the human condition. The human being, in the Gnostic perspective, is the embodiment of this cosmic tension, as he carries in his constitution a divine spark—the most intimate and inalienable portion of the Pleroma—imprisoned in a material body molded by the inferior forces of the Demiurge. Human existence, therefore, transcends simple sensory and psychological experience; it is the enactment of a spiritual drama, where every choice, every awakening, every expanded perception of one's own nature reflects an invisible battle between the luminous forces of the Pleroma and the limiting forces of matter. In this scenario, the field of divine forces is not just a cosmic backdrop, but an internal and external reality that intertwines with the individual destiny of each soul, making the spiritual search for knowledge and liberation not just a philosophical possibility, but an existential necessity to restore the broken primordial unity.

At the same time, this field of divine forces operates as a pedagogical structure of the cosmos itself, where every aspect of reality—from natural phenomena to the deepest intuitions of the soul—can serve as a symbol or sign of a greater process of return to the divine. The luminous spiritual forces, although obscured and fragmented in the material world, never cease to emit signals and invitations to the human soul, encouraging it to remember its true origin and recognize itself as a legitimate heir of the Pleroma. Therefore, spiritual awakening is not an external event, caused by some arbitrary supernatural intervention, but an internal unfolding, a gradual alignment between individual consciousness and the divine flow that permeates the cosmos. In this context, Gnosis emerges not only as esoteric knowledge reserved for a few, but as the living memory of the soul about its own divine identity, a restored memory that dissolves the illusion of separation and reveals the entire universe as a sacred field of reconciliation, where light and shadow, spirit and matter, consciousness and forgetfulness, participate in a single and grand movement of return to the lost unity.

This cosmic conception emphasizes the fundamental duality between spirit and matter, where material reality is perceived as a distorted reflection of the true spiritual essence. Matter, often associated with the Demiurge, is described as a domain of illusion and imprisonment, a field where the divine spark present in humanity remains hidden under layers of ignorance. However, the material world is not completely isolated from the divine; it is permeated by spiritual forces that can serve as bridges to redemption. The Aeons, in this sense, function as intermediaries between humanity and divine fullness, operating as channels through which consciousness can awaken to its true origin. This cosmic structure suggests that salvation does not occur through dogmatic beliefs or obedience to external norms, but rather through the recognition and activation of the inner divine spark, a process that leads to the return to the primordial source of existence.

Within this vision, the field of divine forces is not restricted to a struggle between good and evil in simplistic moral terms, but represents a journey of reintegration and self-knowledge. Humanity, upon recognizing its spiritual nature, begins to play an active role in the recomposition of the cosmic order, transcending the illusion of separation and restoring its connection with the divine. This process is facilitated by Gnosis, the transcendental knowledge that allows the soul to navigate between the spiritual forces that shape reality, discerning what leads to liberation and what keeps the being imprisoned in materiality. Thus, Gnostic cosmology offers a deep and transformative perspective on the universe and the role of the human being within it, highlighting the importance of spiritual awakening as the path to true liberation.

At the heart of Gnostic cosmology lies the concept of the Supreme Divinity, often designated as the Monad, the Ineffable Father, or the Abyss. This primordial Divinity is conceived as absolutely transcendent, unattainable and unknowable to the human mind. It is the ultimate source of all existence, the original principle of all that is, but which remains beyond all description, definition, or limitation. The Monad is not a personal being or a creator in the conventional sense, but rather a fundamental reality, a divine fullness that manifests itself in a gradual and hierarchical manner, giving rise to all things.

From the Monad emanates a continuous and dynamic process of manifestation, known as emanation. In this process, the Supreme Divinity radiates from itself a series of spiritual beings, progressively less pure and less close to the original source. These emanations are the Aeons, the cosmic intelligences and divine forces that populate the Pleroma, the spiritual region of fullness and light that surrounds the Supreme Divinity. The Aeons, although distinct from the Monad, participate in its divine nature and act as intermediaries between the transcendent world and the lower spheres of reality. Emanation is not an act of creation in the sense of producing something from nothing, but rather an expansion of the Divinity itself, a gradual manifestation of its fullness and potentiality.

A central principle of Gnostic cosmology is the fundamental duality between spirit and matter, light and darkness, the transcendent and the immanent. This duality is not merely metaphysical, but also ontological and cosmological. The spiritual world, the Pleroma, is conceived as the realm of light, truth, perfection, and immutability, inhabited by the Aeons and the Supreme Divinity. In contrast, the material world is seen as the realm of darkness, illusion, imperfection, and change, a domain created by an inferior and imperfect entity, the Demiurge.

The Demiurge, a prominent figure in Gnostic cosmology, is not the Supreme Divinity, but rather an inferior emanation, often identified with the God of the Old Testament in some Gnostic traditions. The Demiurge, through ignorance, arrogance, or a deviation from the original divine plan, is said to have created the material world, imprisoning the divine spark, the spirit, in dense and illusory matter. The creation of the material world is, therefore, seen as a cosmic error, a fall from original perfection into imperfection and suffering. The Demiurge, although the creator of the material world, is considered ignorant of the true Supreme Divinity and the higher spiritual dimensions of reality. He governs the material world with restrictive and punitive laws, keeping humanity in a state of ignorance and spiritual captivity.

Within this dualistic cosmology, humanity occupies a paradoxical and complex position. The human being is conceived as composed of two distinct and conflicting natures: a material body, belonging to the world of the Demiurge and subject to corruption and mortality, and a divine spark, the spirit or soul, which comes from the Pleroma and yearns for return to its divine origin. This divine spark, often referred to as "pneuma" in Greek, is the true essence of the human being, his connection with the spiritual world and his capacity to achieve Gnosis, the saving knowledge.

Gnostic cosmology, therefore, is not just a description of the structure of the universe, but also a narrative of the human condition and the path of salvation. The material world, created by the Demiurge, is seen as a place of suffering, ignorance, and spiritual exile. The mission of humanity, or at least of those who possess the awakened divine spark, is to seek Gnosis, the revealing knowledge that liberates the spirit from the prison of matter and leads it back to the Pleroma, to union with the Supreme Divinity. Gnosis is not merely intellectual knowledge, but rather a transformative and intuitive experience, a deep understanding of one's own divine nature and the true destiny of the soul.

To achieve Gnosis, Gnostic cosmology postulates the need for a Savior, a divine messenger sent from the Pleroma to awaken humanity to its true spiritual condition and reveal the path of liberation. Christ, in the Gnostic perspective, is often identified as this Savior, a prominent Aeon who descended to the material world to transmit Gnosis and offer the possibility of redemption. The message of Christ, in the Gnostic context, does not focus so much on the atonement of sins through suffering and death, but rather on the revelation of saving knowledge and the awakening of spiritual consciousness.

Gnostic cosmology, with its radical duality and its pessimistic view of the material world, may seem distant and even strange to the contemporary mentality. However, it is important to recognize that this cosmology reflects a deep concern with human suffering, spiritual alienation, and the search for a transcendent meaning in life. The Gnostic vision of the universe as a field of divine forces, in constant tension between light and darkness, resonates with the human experience of inner conflict, of the search for meaning, and of the yearning for transcendence.

Furthermore, Gnostic cosmology offers an implicit critique of forms of religion that overemphasize the material world and external authority, to the detriment of inner experience and direct knowledge of

God. By valuing Gnosis, mystical experience, and the individual search for spiritual truth, Gnosticism proposes a path of religiosity that is more intimate, transformative, and liberating.

Gnostic cosmology, therefore, represents a complex and multifaceted system of thought, which has influenced various spiritual currents throughout history and which continues to arouse interest and reflection in the contemporary world. By exploring the fundamental principles of Gnostic cosmology, we can broaden our understanding of the history of Christianity, the diversity of religious thought, and the perennial human search for meaning, transcendence, and spiritual liberation. The vision of the universe as a field of divine forces, proposed by Gnostic cosmology, invites us to rethink our relationship with the material world, our spiritual identity, and our ultimate destiny.

# Chapter 4
# Cosmic Intelligences

Understanding cosmic intelligences in the context of esoteric Christianity reveals a sophisticated and living network of spiritual consciousnesses that sustain and permeate the totality of the cosmos, integrating the visible and the invisible in a dynamic tapestry of divine emanations. Each of these intelligences, known as Aeons, emerges from the very substance of the Supreme Divinity, not as externally created entities, but as direct and living extensions of the divine fullness. This conception dissolves the idea of a rigid separation between Creator and creation, replacing it with a vision where the universe is a fluid and hierarchical expression of the divine essence itself in constant self-expression.

In this model, the universe is more than a simple physical space or an arena of events; it is a spiritual organism, where each level of existence reflects a unique combination of light, wisdom, and purpose, filtered through the multiple layers of intelligences that mediate the relationship between the ineffable and the manifest. These cosmic intelligences not only structure the celestial order but also participate directly in the flow of consciousness that permeates every being, connecting the human spirit to the higher dimensions and guiding the awakening of the divine spark present in the depths of each soul.

Throughout Gnostic and esoteric traditions, Aeons are understood not as mere theological symbols or philosophical abstractions, but as real potencies, endowed with intelligence, will, and specific function within the cosmic drama of the fall and redemption. They form chains of emanation, where each Aeon carries and reflects a specific attribute of the Supreme Divinity—be it wisdom, truth, love, power, or light—and, at the same time, collaborates with the other Aeons to maintain the cohesion of the original divine structure. This cosmic interdependence creates a field of intelligent forces that not only sustains the harmony of the Pleroma but also serves as a communication pathway between the divine source and the souls that, even imprisoned in the lower layers of matter, preserve within themselves the echo of these spiritual potencies. This communication, however, is not automatic or guaranteed; it depends on the inner attunement of the human soul, which must learn to recognize the echoes of the Pleroma, progressively tuning itself to the luminous frequencies of the cosmic intelligences, thus awakening its ancestral memory and its natural longing for the return to the divine origin.

These cosmic intelligences, therefore, are not distant or inaccessible figures; they are the very expression of divine intelligence in its continuous operation in the heart of the cosmos and the soul. Each Aeon is a living door that connects the finite to the infinite, a cosmic mirror where the divine contemplates itself in its multiple manifestations. In this sense, the spiritual journey of the Gnostic seeker is, in essence, a journey of recognition and alignment with these primordial potencies, which already inhabit their own being in a latent state. By understanding the nature and function of the Aeons, the seeker discovers that the structure of the universe and the structure of their own soul are reflections of the same spiritual order, and that awakening to this reality is to reactivate the lost link between their innermost essence and the living field of cosmic intelligences. Thus, the knowledge of cosmic intelligences in esoteric Christianity is not just a metaphysical speculation; it is the key to the reintegration of the soul into the original divine flow, rescuing the lost harmony between the human and the sacred.

Within this paradigm, the manifestation of the Aeons occurs through a process of emanation, where each cosmic intelligence emerges as a reflection of the divine fullness and carries with it specific aspects of universal wisdom. This structure not only gives order to the universe but also establishes a link between the divine and humanity, allowing higher knowledge to be accessible to those who seek to understand their true nature. In the Pleroma, the abode of pure spiritual entities, the Aeons form a harmonious system of light and knowledge, interacting with each other to maintain the balance of creation. However, when this balance is disturbed—as occurs in the fall of Sophia, Wisdom—the cosmos experiences a distancing from the original source, giving rise to the illusion of the material world and the need for redemption through Gnosis.

The relationship between the Aeons and humanity transcends the simple concept of worship or devotion. In the esoteric context, these cosmic intelligences not only govern the higher planes but also act as spiritual guides, awakening the divine spark present in each individual. The search for Gnosis, therefore, involves reconnecting with these universal principles, allowing human consciousness to transcend the limitations imposed by the material world and return to the state of unity with the divine. This process does not depend exclusively on faith or belief, but rather on direct experience and intuitive knowledge, which lead to the recognition of spiritual truth. In this way, the exploration of cosmic intelligences within esoteric Christianity not only expands the understanding of the structure of the universe but also reveals paths for inner transformation and the liberation of the soul.

In the philosophical and religious context of late antiquity, the term "aion" was frequently used to designate cosmic periods of great extension or the very ages of the world. In Platonic and Neoplatonic thought, "aion" could refer to timeless eternity, in contrast to the linear and mutable time of the sensible world. This association with eternity and with elevated temporal dimensions is reflected in the use of the term "Aeon" to designate spiritual beings that inhabit higher spheres of reality, existing on a plane of eternity and transcendence.

Within the Gnostic system, Aeons are understood as emanations of the Supreme Divinity, the primordial and unknowable Monad that resides at the apex of the spiritual hierarchy. As emanations, Aeons are not creations in the traditional sense, but rather expansions of the divine essence itself, irradiations of the light and fullness of the Monad. This process of emanation is often described as a cascade of manifestation, where the Supreme Divinity, in its superabundance of being, generates a series of spiritual beings that participate, to varying degrees, in its divine nature. The Aeons, therefore, share the nature of the Monad, but also possess their individuality and specific functions within the cosmic order.

The nature of the Aeons is essentially spiritual and luminous. They inhabit the Pleroma, the region of divine fullness, a realm of light, truth, and perfection that extends beyond the material and chaotic world created by the Demiurge. Aeons are described as cosmic intelligences, divine archetypes, and organizing forces that actively participate in the structure and dynamism of the spiritual cosmos. They are not static or passive entities, but rather living and dynamic forces, imbued with divine consciousness, will, and power.

The characteristics of the Aeons can be understood in several dimensions. First, they are beings of light and wisdom, emanating the luminosity of the Supreme Divinity and possessing a deep knowledge of the laws and mysteries of the spiritual universe. They are the holders of Gnosis, the saving knowledge that frees the soul from the ignorance and illusion of the material world. Second, Aeons are organizing and harmonizing forces of the cosmos. They act to maintain the divine order, balance cosmic energies, and ensure the cohesion and harmony of the Pleroma. They also play a role in the organization of the material world, although indirectly and mediated, seeking to contain the chaos and imperfection inherent in the creation of the Demiurge. Third, Aeons are intermediaries between the Supreme Divinity and humanity. They act as divine messengers, revealing Gnosis to awakened human beings and offering assistance and guidance on the path of spiritual ascension. Christ, in the Gnostic perspective, is often identified as a prominent Aeon, sent to the material world with the mission of revealing Gnosis and guiding humanity back to its divine origin.

The first mentions of the Aeons in the Nag Hammadi texts and the Apocryphal Gospels reveal the central importance of this concept within Gnostic thought. In the Apocryphon of John, one of the most influential texts of Nag Hammadi, the Gnostic cosmogony is narrated in detail, describing the emanation of the Aeons from the Monad, the creation of the Pleroma, and the fall of Sophia, a female Aeon who plays a crucial role in Gnostic cosmogony. In this text, the Aeons are presented as glorious and radiant beings, each with a name and a specific function within the divine hierarchy. Among the Aeons mentioned in the Apocryphon of John, Barbelo, a primordial female Aeon associated with the Monad, Christ, the savior Aeon, and Sophia, the divine wisdom that deviated from the Pleroma, stand out.

In the Gospel of Truth, another fundamental text of Nag Hammadi, the figure of the Aeon Christ is central. This gospel presents Christ as the revealer of Gnosis, the messenger of truth who came to awaken humanity to its true spiritual identity and guide it back to the Father. Although the term "Aeon" is not explicitly used to describe Christ in the Gospel of Truth, the language and themes of the text clearly place him within the context of Aeonic cosmology. Christ is presented as an emanation of the Father, a being of light and truth that transcends the material world and offers salvation through knowledge and love.

In the Apocryphal Gospels, although the concept of Aeons is not always as explicitly developed as in the Nag Hammadi texts, it is possible to find references and ideas that align with Aeonic cosmology. The Gospel of Thomas, for example, with its collection of secret sayings of Jesus, suggests a worldview where spiritual reality is primordial and the material world is seen as transitory and illusory. Although the Aeons are not named directly, the teachings of Jesus in the Gospel of Thomas frequently point to a transcendent dimension and to the importance of self-knowledge and inner searching to reach the truth.

The introduction to the Aeons, therefore, opens up a vast field of exploration within esoteric Christianity. Understanding the nature and functions of the Aeons is fundamental to entering into Gnostic cosmology, its vision of creation, redemption, and human destiny. The Aeons, as cosmic intelligences and organizing forces, represent a dimension of spiritual reality that transcends our everyday perception and invites us to expand our understanding of the divine and the cosmos. The journey through the world of the Aeons is a journey towards the mystery, wisdom, and light that resides in the heart of esoteric Christianity.

# Chapter 5
# Religious and Philosophical Context

The formulation of the concept of Aeons within esoteric Christianity and Gnostic cosmology reflects a sophisticated and innovative synthesis, rooted in a highly dynamic religious and philosophical landscape characteristic of Late Antiquity. This period, marked by the fusion of cultural, philosophical, and spiritual traditions, provided fertile ground for the construction of a cosmological vision that sought to reconcile the absolute transcendence of an ineffable divine principle with the multiplicity of forces operating in the structure and maintenance of the universe. Aeons emerge as answers to this conceptual need: cosmic intelligences that, at the same time, preserve the essential unity of divinity and explain the diversity of spiritual and material manifestations. This proposal did not arise in isolation, but engaged in intense dialogue with Platonism, Neoplatonism, mystical Judaism, and the mystery religions, appropriating symbols, archetypes, and hierarchical schemes already present in the religious and philosophical imaginary of the time.

Platonism, with its division between the sensible world and the intelligible world, provided the conceptual matrix for understanding a higher reality inhabited by eternal and perfect forms, whose imperfect reflections make up the material universe. Gnosticism, by absorbing this division, added a more dramatic spiritual dimension to it, interpreting the material world not only as an imperfect copy, but as a tragic rupture, a departure from divine fullness. In this context, the Aeons assume a central role as mediators between the Pleroma—the spiritual fullness inhabited by luminous emanations—and the material cosmos, deformed and marked by forgetfulness. Each Aeon embodies a specific divine quality and actively participates in the spiritual order that sustains the universe. Neoplatonism, in turn, by developing a web of successive emanations starting from a transcendent and ineffable One, offers a model of dynamic explanation that fits perfectly into the Gnostic vision: from the primordial source flow cosmic intelligences, each one a little further from the original perfection, to the point where matter and time emerge as the extremes of ontological separation.

This conceptual dialogue, however, is not restricted to the universe of Greek philosophy. Judaism and early Christianity also provided essential elements for the construction of the concept of Aeons, especially through the apocalyptic tradition and angelology. The belief in celestial hierarchies, composed of angels and archangels, who serve as intermediaries between God and humanity, offered a functional model for thinking about mediation between spiritual and material spheres. However, while traditional angels are seen as subordinate creatures, Aeons are understood as direct emanations of the divine substance, participating in the very essence of the Supreme Divinity. This distinction is crucial, as it places the Aeons within a cosmic dynamic in which each of them not only serves the divinity, but expresses and prolongs its own nature, functioning as living and conscious reflections of the original divine being. Even so, in some Gnostic texts, the distinction between Aeons and angels becomes fluid, suggesting that, in spiritual practice, the recognition of these spiritual powers does not depend so much on their rigid classification, but on the direct experience of their presences and functions.

The creative synthesis that resulted in the Gnostic concept of Aeons is, therefore, proof of Gnosticism's ability to dialogue with different traditions and reinterpret them in light of its own spiritual vision. Platonic, Neoplatonic, Jewish, Christian, and mystery elements combine in a system that seeks to answer the great spiritual question of the time: how to reconcile the existence of a perfect and transcendent divine principle with the evident imperfection and suffering of the material world. By transforming the Aeons into cosmic intelligences, living forces that organize, illuminate, and sustain the structure of spiritual reality, Gnosticism not only offered an explanatory cosmology, but also built a path of spiritual return. To know the Aeons is not only to understand the universe—it is to recognize, within oneself, the same spiritual powers that make up the Pleroma and to realize that inner awakening is the key to reintegrating into this divine web of light and wisdom, rescuing the forgotten memory of the origin and ultimate destiny of the soul.

In the realm of philosophical influences, Platonism and Neoplatonism emerge as currents of thought of primordial importance for the formation of the concept of Aeons. Platonism, originating in the teachings of Plato, already presented a dualistic worldview, distinguishing between the sensible world, mutable and imperfect, and the intelligible world, eternal and perfect, inhabited by Forms or Ideas, perfect archetypes of all things existing in the sensible world. Neoplatonism, developed from Platonism from the 3rd century AD onwards, deepened this dualistic vision, hierarchizing reality in a scale of emanations from a supreme and one principle, the One, which resembles the Gnostic Monad. In this Neoplatonic hierarchy, the successive emanations of the One, called hypostases, represent different levels of reality, progressively less perfect and more distant from the original source. The Gnostic Aeons can be understood as entities analogous to the Neoplatonic hypostases, intermediaries between the Supreme Divinity and the material world, manifestations of divine intelligence and will in different degrees of proximity to the One/Monad.

The Neoplatonic influence is particularly evident in the description of the Gnostic Pleroma, the dwelling place of the Aeons, which echoes the Neoplatonic conception of the intelligible world, a realm of light, intelligence, and perfection that transcends the sensible world. The idea of emanation, central to both Neoplatonism and Gnosticism, also reinforces this connection, suggesting a process of gradual and hierarchical manifestation from an original principle.

Neoplatonic philosophers such as Plotinus and Proclus explored in detail the nature of emanations and the hierarchical structure of the universe, offering a conceptual framework that certainly influenced the development of Gnostic Aeonic cosmology.

In addition to philosophical influences, the concept of Aeons also finds parallels in various religious and mythological traditions of Late Antiquity, especially in Hellenism and the mystery religions. Hellenism, the predominant culture and religion in the Mediterranean world after the conquests of Alexander the Great, was characterized by a religious syncretism, a mixture of elements from Greek, Eastern, and Egyptian traditions. In this syncretic context, various deities and spiritual entities were venerated, often associated with cosmic forces and temporal cycles. The mystery religions, such as the Eleusinian mysteries, the Mithraic mysteries, and the mysteries of Isis, offered initiation rituals and secret teachings that promised initiates salvation and immortality through knowledge and mystical experience.

In the Hellenistic context and the mystery religions, it is possible to identify entities and concepts that bear similarities to the Gnostic Aeons. Deities such as Hecate, Hermes Trismegistus, Mithras, and Isis were often associated with hidden wisdom, esoteric knowledge, and mediation between the divine world and the human world. The notions of celestial hierarchies, of divine intermediaries, and of cosmic forces that govern human destiny were also common in these traditions. The initiation rituals of the mystery religions, with their symbolism of death and rebirth, of descent into the underworld and ascension to the light, can be seen as parallels to the Gnostic soul's journey in search of Gnosis and the return to the Pleroma.

The relationship between the Aeons and the concept of angels and archangels in Judaism and early Christianity is a crucial point for understanding the specificity of the Gnostic vision. In Judaism and Christianity, the belief in angelic beings as messengers and helpers of God was already well established in the period of Late Antiquity. Angels and archangels were seen as spiritual entities that populate the heavens, execute the divine will, and intercede on behalf of humanity. Names of archangels such as Michael, Gabriel, Raphael, and Uriel were already familiar in Judaism and were incorporated into early Christianity.

However, the Gnostic conception of the Aeons differs in important aspects from the Judeo-Christian view of angels and archangels. While angels and archangels are generally seen as creations of God, servants of his will, and subordinate to his authority, the Aeons are conceived as emanations of the Supreme Divinity itself, participating in its divine nature and sharing, to a certain extent, in its autonomy and power. The Aeons are not mere messengers, but rather cosmic forces and divine intelligences that act in the organization and evolution of the spiritual and material universe.

Furthermore, the Gnostic Aeonic hierarchy is much more complex and elaborate than the Judeo-Christian angelic hierarchy. The Gnostic Pleroma is populated by a vast range of Aeons, each with a name, a function, and a specific role within the divine order. The relationships between the Aeons, their genealogies, and their attributes are explored in detail in the Gnostic texts, revealing a sophisticated and multifaceted cosmological system. While Judeo-Christian angelology focuses primarily on the role of angels as intermediaries between God and humanity, Gnostic Aeonology encompasses a broader vision, involving the organization of the spiritual cosmos, the dynamics of divine emanation, and the process of redemption of the human soul.

Despite these differences, it is important to recognize that the concept of Aeons can also be seen as a re-elaboration and expansion of pre-existing ideas about intermediary spiritual beings present in Judaism and early Christianity. The influence of Jewish and Christian angelology on the development of Gnostic Aeonology is undeniable, especially with regard to the idea of celestial hierarchies and spiritual entities that act as divine messengers and helpers. In some Gnostic texts, such as the Gospel of Mary Magdalene, a certain indistinction between the terms "Aeon" and "angel" can be observed, suggesting an overlap and continuity between the two categories of spiritual beings.

The insertion of the Aeons in the religious and philosophical context of Late Antiquity reveals their syncretic nature and their ability to integrate and transform ideas and concepts from various sources. Gnosticism, and the concept of Aeons in particular, can be seen as a creative synthesis of elements from

Platonism, Neoplatonism, Hellenistic mystery religions, Judaism, and early Christianity. This synthesis resulted in an original and complex worldview, which offered an alternative answer to the fundamental questions about the origin of the universe, the nature of the divine, human destiny, and the path of salvation. Understanding the Aeons in the context of Late Antiquity allows us to appreciate the richness and diversity of religious and philosophical thought of this era, and the human capacity to create new forms of spirituality and worldview from a dynamic dialogue between different traditions and ideas.

# Chapter 6
# The Divine Fullness

A deep understanding of the Pleroma reveals a spiritual dimension that precedes any material conception and expresses the absolute essence of the Supreme Divinity in its purest and most abundant form. This spiritual realm transcends any idea of physical or spatial locality and manifests as a full state of existence, where the primordial, incorruptible, and eternal light constitutes the essential substance of all divine reality. The Pleroma, therefore, cannot be reduced to an abstract or symbolic concept, but is configured as the very expression of divine completeness, where each element participates integrally in the unique and transcendent essence of the primordial Monad. This spiritual fullness is not static or inert, but dynamic and alive, a constant pulsation of the divine presence that emanates, sustains, and leads all things back to their immaculate origin. In the heart of this realm of light, truth, and perfection, the Aeons arise as direct manifestations of the infinite richness and creative power of the Supreme Divinity, each carrying within itself a unique facet of divine wisdom and love. Each Aeon is a living expression of fullness, and together, they form a sacred tapestry that reflects the totality of the divine being in its multiple possibilities of manifestation.

The emanation of these spiritual beings is not an isolated or casual event, but reflects an ordered process, where the divine fullness overflows spontaneously and naturally, without rupture or separation, but rather as a continuous extension of the divine essence itself. Just as the light of a star fills the space around it without losing connection with its source, the Aeons arise as rays that, although distinct, remain rooted in the heart of the Monad, participating in its luminous and eternal nature. Each emanation carries within it not only the substance of divine light, but also primordial wisdom, cosmic harmony, and creative power, reflecting the ordering intelligence that permeates the entire Pleroma. This hierarchical progression of emanations does not imply distance or weakening of the divine essence, but reveals the infinite richness of the source, whose fullness is never exhausted, even when multiplying into countless spiritual forms. In this incessant flow of emanations, the Pleroma reveals itself as the stage where the divine itself self-knows and self-transcends, expanding in layers of light and wisdom, each revealing hidden and wonderful aspects of the infinite fullness of the Supreme Divinity.

Within this context, the understanding of the Pleroma cannot be dissociated from the direct spiritual experience and the inner search for saving knowledge — Gnosis — which leads the human soul back to its true abode. The Pleroma represents the supreme archetype of perfection and spiritual happiness, the primordial model of harmony and truth that reflects the ultimate destiny of every divine spark exiled in material creation. In its bosom, there is no absence, lack, or conflict, for each element finds its full realization in harmonious communion with the whole. This state of unity does not nullify individuality, but elevates it to its most perfect expression, where each Aeon, each being, and each spiritual spark becomes a luminous mirror of the Supreme Divinity itself. This vision of the Pleroma as the absolute divine fullness, where light, wisdom, love, and truth intertwine in an eternal dance of self-discovery and cosmic celebration, offers not only a key to Gnostic cosmology, but an invitation to a profound inner transformation, in which the soul, upon recognizing its origin and destiny in the Pleroma, awakens to its true spiritual identity and aligns itself with the eternal flow of divine emanation.

The Pleroma is conceived as the dwelling place of the Supreme Divinity, the primordial and unknowable Monad that resides at the apex of the spiritual hierarchy. It is the realm of uncreated light, the source of all existence, and the originating principle of all things. The Pleroma is not a physical or spatially delimited place, but rather a state of being, a dimension of reality that transcends the spatio-temporal categories of the material world. It is a spiritual, vibrant, and dynamic reality, filled with the divine presence and inhabited by a myriad of spiritual beings, the Aeons.

The process of emanation of the Aeons from the Supreme Divinity is a central concept of Gnostic cosmology. As already mentioned, emanation is not an act of creation in the traditional sense, but rather an expansion of the divine essence itself, an irradiation of the fullness and superabundance of the Monad. The Supreme Divinity, in its overflowing nature, manifests itself in a gradual and hierarchical manner, generating a series of spiritual beings that participate, in varying degrees, in its divinity. The Aeons are, therefore, considered emanations of the Monad, projections of its light and wisdom in the realm of the Pleroma.

The emanation of the Aeons can be compared to a source of light that radiates its rays in all directions. The source, the Monad, remains inexhaustible and unchanged, even while emanating its light. The rays, the Aeons, are distinct from the source, but still participate in its luminous nature and transmit its light. Emanation is a continuous and dynamic process, an expression of the vitality and fecundity of the Supreme Divinity.

The luminous and spiritual nature of the Pleroma is emphasized in various Gnostic texts. The Pleroma is described as a realm of intense and radiant light, a sea of divine luminosity that fills all spiritual space. This light is not the physical light of the material world, but rather a spiritual light, pure and incorruptible, that emanates from the very essence of the Supreme Divinity. The Aeons, as inhabitants of the Pleroma, are also beings of light, radiant and glorious, manifesting the divine luminosity in their own natures and irradiations.

The Pleroma is not only a realm of light, but also a realm of fullness and perfection. In it, all things exist in their perfect and archetypal form, free from the limitations, imperfection, and corruption that characterize the material world. The Pleroma is the abode of eternal truth, infinite wisdom, and divine love. It is a complete and self-sufficient state of being, where there is no lack, suffering, or want. The fullness of the Pleroma contrasts sharply with the emptiness and want of the material world, created by the Demiurge from ignorance and illusion.

The emanation of the Aeons from the Pleroma is not a random or chaotic process, but rather an ordered and hierarchical process. The Aeons are organized into complex families and hierarchies, reflecting the order and harmony of the divine realm. Some Aeons are considered primary, closer to the Monad and of greater power and importance, while others are secondary, tertiary, and so on, forming a vast and intricate network of relationships and interconnections within the Pleroma. This Aeonic hierarchy does not imply a hierarchy of value or moral superiority, but rather a differentiation of functions and attributes within the divine order.

The emanation of the Aeons from the Pleroma can also be understood as a process of self-knowledge and self-development of the Supreme Divinity. By emanating the Aeons, the Monad manifests its own inner richness, its infinite potentiality, and its intrinsic complexity. Each Aeon, in its individuality and specificity, represents an aspect of the Supreme Divinity, a facet of its multifaceted nature. The totality of the Aeons, the Pleroma in its fullness, reflects the totality of the Supreme Divinity, its infinite and inscrutable essence.

The understanding of the Pleroma and the emanation of the Aeons is fundamental to Gnostic cosmology and esoteric Christian spirituality. The Pleroma represents the ultimate goal of the spiritual journey, the realm of fullness and light to which the human soul longs to return. Gnosis, the saving knowledge, is the path that leads the soul back to the Pleroma, freeing it from the illusion of the material world and reuniting it with its divine origin. The Aeons, as inhabitants of the Pleroma and emanations of the Supreme Divinity, act as guides and helpers on this journey, offering wisdom, protection, and inspiration to spiritual seekers.

The image of the Pleroma as a realm of light, fullness, and perfection, and the understanding of the emanation of the Aeons as a dynamic and hierarchical process, offer a rich panorama for contemplation and meditation. Visualizing the Pleroma as a sea of radiant light, inhabited by glorious spiritual beings, can inspire the soul to rise above the limitations of the material world and aspire to union with the divine. Contemplating the emanation of the Aeons as an expression of the superabundance and fecundity of the Supreme Divinity can awaken a sense of reverence and gratitude for the infinite generosity of the primordial source.

The exploration of the concept of the Pleroma and the emanation of the Aeons invites us to expand our vision of reality, to recognize the existence of spiritual dimensions that transcend our everyday perception, and to seek a deeper and more meaningful connection with the divine. The Pleroma, as the dwelling place of divine fullness, represents a spiritual ideal, an archetype of perfection and happiness that can inspire our inner journey and guide our search for Gnosis and union with the Supreme Divinity. The understanding of the emanation of the Aeons offers us a key to unlocking the mysteries of Gnostic cosmology and grasping the richness and complexity of esoteric Christianity.

# Chapter 7
# Aeonic Hierarchy

Within the luminous and ordered fullness of the Pleroma, the existence and function of the Aeons unfold in an intricate web of carefully organized relationships and roles, where each spiritual being not only manifests an aspect of the Supreme Divinity but also actively and harmoniously collaborates in the sustenance of the divine order. The Pleroma, far from being an undifferentiated or chaotic space, reveals itself as a living spiritual structure, where the very fullness of the primordial Monad is expressed in hierarchical layers that reflect, at each level, divine wisdom, light, and purpose. Each Aeon occupies a specific place in this great spiritual organism, not as a matter of power or supremacy, but according to the particularity of its essence and the nature of its spiritual gift. Thus, the Aeonic hierarchy is not configured as a scale of value or merit, but as a symphony of complementary functions, where each Aeon is called to manifest, preserve, and radiate a fragment of divine truth, collaborating in the preservation of the cosmic harmony that permeates the Pleroma.

In the dynamics of this spiritual cosmos, the relationships between the Aeons draw a map of living connections, where proximity to the primordial Monad determines the intensity of the divine light that each being is capable of radiating. The Aeons closest to the original source of all light and wisdom vibrate at frequencies of greater purity and potency, while the Aeons situated in more external layers act as bridges and intermediaries, channeling the primordial light to more distant regions of the Pleroma and, eventually, beyond its spiritual borders. This decentralization of the divine fullness does not imply a weakening or dilution of the light, but a progressive adjustment of the intensity of the divine presence according to the receptive capacity of each sphere and each being. This layered structure allows the infinite fullness of the Monad to be revealed in an orderly and accessible way, respecting the diversity of functions and the richness of manifestations that make up the great spiritual body of the Pleroma. The continuous flow of light and wisdom between the different levels of the Aeonic hierarchy is not a mechanical or imposing movement, but an expression of divine love that incessantly seeks to share its own essence with all levels of spiritual creation.

The hierarchical ordering of the Pleroma, sustained by this network of relationships between the Aeons, not only guarantees the stability and harmony of the spiritual cosmos but also offers a path of ascension and reintegration for spiritual consciousnesses that are temporarily distanced from the divine fullness. Each Aeon, in its specific function, not only preserves and manifests a portion of divine truth but also acts as a guide, a mirror, and a source of inspiration for souls on a journey back to the primordial light. In this sense, the Aeonic hierarchy is not a barrier or limitation, but a living ladder, where each step reveals a new layer of wisdom and light, inviting each conscious being to deepen their understanding and expand their own capacity to reflect and contain the divine presence. Thus, understanding the Aeonic hierarchy is not just an exercise in metaphysical mapping, but a spiritual key to the reintegration of the soul, an invitation for each seeker of Gnosis to recognize their intimate connection with this vast spiritual network and accept their own place and their own vocation within the divine order, actively participating in the great work of manifestation and revelation of the infinite fullness of the Supreme Divinity.

The hierarchical structure of the Aeons can be understood on several levels. At a fundamental level, the Aeons can be grouped into families or sets, often referred to as "syzygies" or "conjugations" in Gnostic texts. These Aeonic families represent units of divine consciousness and energy, usually composed of a pair of complementary Aeons, one masculine and one feminine, which together manifest a particular aspect of the Supreme Divinity. The idea of the syzygy reflects the duality present in Gnostic cosmology, but also its search for unity and the reconciliation of opposites. The union of the Aeonic syzygy represents fullness and perfection, the complete manifestation of a divine principle.

Among the most prominent Aeonic families mentioned in Gnostic texts, the first syzygy stands out, often composed of the primordial Monad, the Ineffable

Father, and his feminine counterpart, usually called Barbelo or Ennoia (Thought). This first syzygy represents the root of all Aeonic emanation, the starting point of the manifestation of the Supreme Divinity in the Pleroma. From this first union, other syzygies emanate, each manifesting specific attributes and functions within the divine order.

Another important Aeonic syzygy is that of Christ and Sophia. Christ, in the Gnostic context, is often understood as a savior Aeon, sent from the Pleroma to reveal Gnosis to humanity and guide it back to its divine origin. Sophia, the Divine Wisdom, is a complex and multifaceted feminine Aeon, whose story and destiny play a crucial role in Gnostic cosmogony. The syzygy of Christ and Sophia represents the union of divine wisdom and the redemptive principle, the manifestation of light and truth that dispels the ignorance and illusion of the material world.

In addition to syzygies, the Aeons are also organized into broader hierarchies, forming orders and levels of manifestation within the Pleroma. Some Aeons are considered primary, occupying positions of prominence and authority in the divine hierarchy, while others are secondary, tertiary, and so on, forming a vast and intricate network of spiritual beings. The primary Aeons, closest to the Monad, radiate a greater intensity of divine light and exert a more direct influence on the lower spheres of reality. The secondary and tertiary Aeons act as intermediaries and auxiliaries, transmitting the energy and wisdom of the higher Aeons to the more distant regions of the Pleroma and to the material world.

It is important to emphasize that the Aeonic hierarchy is not rigid or static, but rather dynamic and fluid. The relationships between the Aeons are characterized by cooperation, interdependence, and the constant flow of energy and information. The Aeons do not compete with each other for power or status, but rather collaborate in harmony for the realization of the divine plan and for the maintenance of cosmic order. The Aeonic hierarchy reflects the order and organization inherent in the spiritual universe, but also its vitality and dynamism.

The relationship between the primary and secondary Aeons can be compared to the relationship between a central sun and the planets that orbit it. The sun, the Monad, or the primary Aeons, emits light and energy that sustain and illuminate the planets, the secondary and tertiary Aeons. The planets, in turn, reflect and distribute the sun's light, transmitting its energy to the most distant regions of the solar system, the Pleroma. This image illustrates the interdependence and complementarity between the different levels of the Aeonic hierarchy.

Exploring the families and relationships within the divine Aeonic realm also involves considering the figure of specific Aeons and their particular functions. Sophia, as mentioned, plays a crucial role in Gnostic cosmogony, being associated with divine wisdom and also with the cosmic fall that resulted in the creation of the material world. Christ, the savior Aeon, is central to Gnostic soteriology, offering Gnosis and the path of redemption. The Holy Spirit, in some Gnostic traditions, is also conceived as a feminine Aeon, associated with vital force, inspiration, and the manifestation of the divine presence in the world.

Other prominent Aeons in Gnostic texts include Autogenes (Self-Generated), Logos (Word), Zoe (Life), Anthropos (Man), Church, and many others. Each of these Aeons possesses specific attributes and functions, contributing to the richness and complexity of the Pleroma. Studying the genealogy and relationships between these Aeons is a fascinating exercise to unravel the mysteries of Gnostic cosmology and to understand the intricate web of consciousnesses and energies that populate the divine realm.

Understanding the Aeonic hierarchy is not just an intellectual exercise or a theological curiosity. It has profound implications for Christian esoteric spirituality and for the inner journey of the seeker of Gnosis. Recognizing the existence of a hierarchy of spiritual beings that act as intermediaries between the Supreme Divinity and humanity can inspire a sense of reverence and admiration for the cosmic order and the richness of the divine realm. Seeking connection with the Aeons, through meditation, contemplation, and prayer, can open channels of communication with cosmic intelligences and allow access to the wisdom and spiritual guidance that emanate from the Pleroma.

The Aeonic hierarchy, with its families, orders, and relationships, represents a map of the spiritual universe, a guide for the soul's journey in search of union with the divine. By exploring this map, the spiritual seeker can orient themselves in the more subtle dimensions of reality, discern the different spiritual energies and influences, and deepen their understanding of their own divine nature and their place in the cosmos. The contemplation of the Aeonic hierarchy can, therefore, be a path to Gnosis, to self-knowledge, and to the transformation of consciousness. The richness and complexity of the Aeonic hierarchy reflect the infinite creativity and intrinsic order of the spiritual universe, inviting the human soul to awaken to its true divine nature and to aspire to the return to the fullness of the Pleroma.

# Chapter 8
# The Cosmic Fall

Sophia's trajectory within the Pleroma and her subsequent fall beyond the luminous boundaries of the divine realm represent a cosmic drama of immense depth, whose implications resonate in every aspect of spiritual and material existence. Sophia, in her most essential nature, embodies the very principle of Divine Wisdom, a living and active intelligence that incessantly seeks to delve into the mysteries of the original source of all light and being. Emanated from the fullness of the Supreme Monad, Sophia is not merely a passive guardian of eternal wisdom, but a vibrant, restless, and creative force, driven by a deep impulse to know, generate, and understand. This unique characteristic makes Sophia a singular figure among the Aeons, for in her the innate luminosity of divine wisdom and the burning flame of the desire to go beyond what is already manifest are merged, exploring territories of being and knowledge not yet revealed. This thirst for expansion, however, leads her to a delicate boundary—the threshold between the harmony of the Pleroma and the dark regions of the primordial void, where the divine light has not yet radiated its order and beauty.

Sophia's movement towards this threshold is not an act of rebellion or deliberate rupture with the divine order, but the manifestation of an impulse inherent in the very dynamism of creative wisdom, which incessantly seeks to know its deepest origins and express its fecundity in new forms. By directing her attention and desire to the unattainable source of the Monad itself, Sophia encounters the ultimate mystery of the Supreme Divinity—a reality so vast and inscrutable that even the Aeons cannot contemplate it directly without losing themselves in its infinity. By extending herself beyond the perfect balance of the Pleroma, Sophia crosses an ontological threshold, entering regions of indistinction and chaos, where the light of the Monad weakens and spiritual powers become unstable. This movement, motivated by the thirst to understand and embrace the fullness of the Monad in its totality, results in a fragmentation of Sophia herself, whose luminous aspects remain anchored in the Pleroma, while her lower parts slide into spheres of increasing density and separation.

Sophia's fall instigates a disturbance that reverberates throughout the spiritual fabric of the Pleroma, triggering a movement of rebalancing that culminates in the manifestation of a completely new reality: the realm of matter and finitude. Separated from the luminous fullness of her origin, Sophia finds herself enveloped in layers of obscurity and confusion, her creative faculties giving shape to an imperfect projection of the divine order—the material cosmos. This involuntary emanation, marked by the lack of the original light, generates the Demiurge, a creative entity blind to its own spiritual origin, who builds the material world as a distorted replica of the spiritual harmony of the Pleroma. Matter, in this context, is not merely a passive substance, but the record of Sophia's anguish, the memory of her longing for the lost light and her desperate attempt to rediscover the original harmony through creation. Each element of the sensible world carries within it the echo of fragmented divine wisdom, as well as the mark of separation and forgetfulness, establishing the existential condition of exile and alienation that defines humanity.

Even in the midst of darkness and the fall, Sophia is never abandoned by the divine fullness. The Pleroma, in its infinite compassion, mobilizes the emanation of a redemptive Aeon—the Christ—whose mission is to restore the connection between Sophia and her luminous origin. The Gnostic Christ, distinct from the historical and dogmatic figure, does not arise as an external savior, but as the very expression of the primordial light descending into the regions of separation to awaken the memory of the divine origin in Sophia and, by extension, in all material creation. Sophia's drama thus becomes the cosmic mirror of the human condition: just as she was lost amidst the desire to understand and create, each human soul, bearer of a spark of the Sophianic light, carries within it the forgotten memory of the Pleroma and the irrepressible longing to return to fullness. Sophia's redemption and the liberation of the human soul become two inseparable aspects of the same divine work, and the awakening of Gnosis represents both the reintegration of fragmented wisdom and the ascension of the soul to its rightful place in the luminous dwelling of the Supreme Divinity.

Sophia, in her primordial essence, is an Aeon of light and wisdom, emanated from the Supreme Divinity and inhabitant of the Pleroma. She is the personification of Divine Wisdom, the cosmic intelligence that permeates the entire spiritual realm and reflects the mind and knowledge of the Monad. Sophia is associated with primordial gnosis, the intuitive and direct knowledge of divine truth, and the ability to discern the mysteries of the universe. In some Gnostic traditions, Sophia is also seen as the divine feminine principle, the female counterpart of the Monad or the Ineffable Father, complementing the primordial duality present in Gnostic cosmology. As an Aeon of wisdom, Sophia possesses a deep understanding of the laws and order of the Pleroma, and actively participates in the harmony and organization of the divine realm. Her luminous nature radiates wisdom and discernment, guiding the other Aeons and illuminating the lower spiritual spheres.

However, Sophia's story is not limited to her divine and luminous nature. One of the central myths of Gnosticism narrates the fall of Sophia, a dramatic cosmic event that is said to have triggered the creation of the material world and the condition of spiritual exile of humanity. The narrative of Sophia's fall varies in detail depending on the different Gnostic strands, but the central theme remains constant: Sophia, moved by a desire to know the unknowable or to create something on her own, is said to have moved away from the

Pleroma or acted independently of the divine will, resulting in a disturbance in the cosmic order and her own fall to the lower regions of reality.

In some versions of the myth, Sophia's fall is described as an act of passion or ardent desire to know the Monad in its totality, a longing that exceeds the limits allowed to the Aeons. In this impetuous desire for knowledge, Sophia is said to have ventured beyond the limits of the Pleroma, losing contact with the divine light and plunging into darkness and chaos. In other versions, Sophia's fall is attributed to a desire for independent creation, an urge to generate something new on her own, without the participation or permission of the Supreme Divinity. In this act of self-affirmation, Sophia is said to have separated herself from the harmony of the Pleroma, giving rise to an imperfect and chaotic emanation, which would become the basis of the material world.

The consequences of Sophia's fall are vast and profound, reverberating throughout the Gnostic cosmos. The disturbance caused by her fall is said to have broken the harmony of the Pleroma, generating a shadow or darkness within the divine fullness. From this disturbance, the Demiurge is said to have emerged, an imperfect entity ignorant of the true Supreme Divinity, who would become the creator of the material world. The material world, therefore, is seen as an indirect consequence of Sophia's fall, an imperfect and chaotic creation, distant from the light and perfection of the Pleroma. Matter, in Gnostic cosmology, is often associated with darkness, illusion, and suffering, reflecting the original disturbance caused by Sophia's fall.

Sophia's fall also has direct implications for the human condition. According to the Gnostic myth, the divine spark, the human spirit or soul, is seen as a particle of Sophia herself, imprisoned in the dense and illusory matter of the material world. The human soul, therefore, carries within it the nostalgia of the Pleroma, the memory of its divine origin and the longing for the return to its primordial dwelling. The human condition is seen as a state of spiritual exile, of ignorance and suffering, resulting from Sophia's fall and the creation of the material world by the Demiurge.

However, Sophia's story does not end with her fall. In the Gnostic myth, Sophia, although she has fallen to the lower regions of reality, is not abandoned by the Supreme Divinity. The Pleroma, in its compassion and wisdom, sends the Aeon Christ to rescue Sophia and restore the cosmic order. Christ, as the revealer of Gnosis, descends into the material world to awaken humanity to its true spiritual identity and to offer the path of redemption and return to the Pleroma. Redemption, in the Gnostic perspective, implies not only the liberation of the human soul from the prison of matter, but also the restoration of Sophia herself and the reunification of the spiritual cosmos.

Sophia, therefore, emerges as a complex and multifaceted figure, who personifies both divine wisdom and the possibility of fall, error, and redemption. She is a symbol of the human soul in its spiritual journey, representing the longing for truth, the search for knowledge, and the experience of exile and return. Sophia's story resonates with the human experience of seeking knowledge, making mistakes, suffering the consequences of choices, and finding redemption and restoration.

Sophia can also be interpreted as a symbol of the divine feminine principle, of the creative and intuitive force that resides in the heart of the Supreme Divinity. Her fall and redemption can be seen as a metaphor for the journey of divine feminine energy through the spheres of reality, from the fullness of the Pleroma to the density of the material world, and back to union with the divine. The figure of Sophia, in her complexity and depth, offers a rich field for reflection on the nature of the feminine, the search for wisdom, and the path of spiritual redemption.

In art and iconography, Sophia is often represented as a majestic and melancholic female figure, often associated with symbols of wisdom, such as books, scrolls, or stars. Her facial expression can convey both the beauty and serenity of divine wisdom and the sadness and longing for her condition of exile. Some representations of Sophia show her falling from the Pleroma, enveloped in darkness and chaos, while others portray her being rescued by Christ or ascending back to the divine light. These artistic representations seek to capture the complexity and richness of the myth of Sophia, visually expressing her divine nature, her cosmic fall, and her quest for redemption.

The exploration of the figure of Sophia, Divine Wisdom, invites us to contemplate the depths of Gnostic cosmology and to reflect on the mysteries of the human condition. Sophia, in her fall and redemption, personifies the journey of the soul in search of Gnosis, the longing for divine truth, and the hope of return to the fullness of the Pleroma. Her story resonates with our own spiritual quest, with our own challenges, and with our own ability to find light and wisdom even in the darkest regions of existence. Sophia, the fallen and redeemed Aeon, remains a powerful and inspiring symbol of the human spiritual journey and the eternal search for union with the divine.

# Chapter 9
# Christ the Savior Aeon

Christ, as the Savior Aeon, manifests as a direct emanation of the divine fullness, a pure expression of the primordial light projected within the Pleroma and destined to act as an essential link between the perfect and spiritual reality and the fragmented and material creation. His origin, distinct from any historical or merely earthly conception, resides in the very essence of the Supreme Monad, where he arises as the creative Word, the living expression of divine thought and a direct reflection of the ordering intelligence that permeates the spiritual cosmos. In the Pleroma, Christ is not just one among the Aeons, but the one in whom the primordial unity and the diversity of emanations are synthesized and harmonized. He is the bearer of the integrating consciousness that encompasses wisdom, love, and divine will, acting as the dynamic axis that sustains cosmic order and preserves the flow of light between the Monad and its emanations. His mission, however, is not restricted to maintaining the internal harmony of the Pleroma, but expands in active compassion, turning to the lower regions where the light has been obscured and spiritual consciousness has fallen into forgetfulness and exile.

Christ's descent into the material world represents an act of cosmic sacrifice, a voluntary choice to cross the layers of density and illusion that separate the Pleroma from the deformed creation, to bring back the light of saving knowledge to those who, forgetful of their divine origin, wander amidst ignorance and suffering. This descent does not imply a limitation or loss of his spiritual nature, for, as an Aeon, Christ remains intrinsically connected to the primordial source of his emanation. While traversing the lower regions, he preserves intact his connection with the fullness, thus being the living bridge between luminous eternity and the fragmented time of matter. He manifests as the revealer of forgotten truth, the one who reminds imprisoned souls of their true name, their spiritual lineage, and the path of return to the Pleroma. This revelation is not merely doctrinal or moral, but existential and experiential: Christ awakens the divine spark dormant in each soul, activating the deep memory of primordial light and rekindling the desire for reintegration and spiritual ascension.

Christ's action as Savior Aeon transcends any isolated mission in time or space and presents itself as a constant and eternal function within the divine economy. His role as mediator and spiritual guide unfolds continuously, not only in the instructions transmitted directly to spiritual disciples, but through a subtle and inner presence that accompanies each soul that awakens to the reality of Gnosis. He is the inner master who whispers the forgotten truth, the luminous beacon that attracts fragmented consciousness back to the original unity. His saving action is inseparable from the very structure of the Gnostic cosmos, for wherever there is a trapped spark, there also pulses the silent and compassionate presence of Christ, offering the key to liberating knowledge. Christ, as an Aeon, embodies the eternal promise of reconciliation between fallen Sophia and the supreme Monad, between matter and spirit, between ignorance and full wisdom. His mission is not exhausted in a historical event or a past revelation, but resonates continuously in each soul that, recognizing its origin and condition of exile, begins the journey of return, guided by the light of the Savior Aeon.

Within the Aeonic hierarchy, Christ occupies a prominent position, although his exact placement varies depending on the different Gnostic schools and systems. In general, Christ is considered a primary Aeon, emanated directly from the Monad or one of the first divine syzygies. His celestial origin and divine nature fundamentally distinguish him from ordinary humanity, placing him on a higher level of spiritual existence. Christ, as an Aeon, inhabits the Pleroma, the realm of light and divine fullness, sharing the eternal and immutable nature of superior spiritual beings. His descent into the material world, therefore, represents a singular and extraordinary event, an act of divine condescension motivated by love and compassion for humanity imprisoned in ignorance and illusion.

The primary role of Christ as an Aeon is that of revealer of Gnosis. In the Gnostic perspective, humanity is in a state of forgetfulness of its true spiritual nature and divine origin. Imprisoned in the material world, created by the imperfect Demiurge, the human soul ignores its own luminous essence and its ultimate destiny in the Pleroma. Christ, as divine messenger, descends to the world to awaken the sleeping souls, to transmit Gnosis, the saving knowledge that frees from ignorance and reconnects with the Supreme Divinity. The Gnosis revealed by Christ is not merely intellectual knowledge or a theoretical doctrine, but rather a transformative and intuitive experience, a direct and experiential knowledge of spiritual truth. It is a knowledge that illuminates the mind, ignites the heart, and awakens consciousness to the divine reality that transcends the material world.

The message of Christ, in the Gnostic perspective, centers on spiritual liberation and self-knowledge. He does not primarily preach an external morality or a set of rules and precepts, but rather a path of inner transformation that leads to Gnosis and redemption. The teachings of Christ, preserved in the Apocryphal Gospels and the Nag Hammadi texts, emphasize the importance of knowing oneself, of recognizing the inner divine spark, and of awakening to the spiritual reality that resides in every human being. Salvation, for Gnosticism, is not achieved through blind faith or dogmatic obedience, but through illuminating knowledge, the Gnosis that frees the soul from ignorance and leads it back to its divine origin.

Christ as Aeon is not only a revealer of Gnosis, but also a guide on the spiritual path. He not only transmits saving knowledge, but also offers the example and assistance necessary for awakened souls to travel the journey of return to the Pleroma. Christ, through his teachings and his spiritual presence, illuminates the path of Gnosis, showing the steps to be taken, the obstacles to be overcome, and the virtues to be cultivated. He is the shepherd who guides the lost sheep back to the fold, the master who leads the disciples to enlightenment, the friend who accompanies fellow travelers in the search for truth. Christ's role as guide manifests both through his explicit teachings, preserved in the Gnostic texts, and through his continuous spiritual presence, which accompanies and supports those who dedicate themselves to the pursuit of Gnosis.

It is important to distinguish the figure of the Aeonic Christ from the conception of the historical Christ and the Christ of orthodox faith. While orthodox Christianity emphasizes the historical humanity of Jesus, his sacrificial death on the cross for the atonement of humanity's sins, and his bodily resurrection as proof of his divinity, Gnosticism offers a different perspective. For Gnosticism, the Aeonic dimension of Christ is primordial, and his historical manifestation in the material world is seen as a secondary and instrumental event for the revelation of Gnosis. The crucifixion and resurrection of Jesus, although not denied, are reinterpreted symbolically, as stages of a process of spiritual initiation and transcendence of the limited human condition. The focus of Gnosticism is not so much on the historicity of Jesus, but rather on the spiritual message and the redemptive power of the Aeon Christ.

The Nag Hammadi texts offer diverse perspectives on the Aeon Christ, enriching and complexifying his figure. The Gospel of Truth presents Christ as the revealer of the Father, the messenger of love and truth who came to dispel ignorance and reconcile humanity with the Supreme Divinity. The Gospel of Philip explores the Gnostic sacraments and the mystical union with Christ as a path to Gnosis. The Apocryphon of John describes the celestial origin of Christ, his emanation from the Pleroma, and his mission to rescue Sophia and humanity. The Gospel of Mary Magdalene presents dialogues between the resurrected Jesus and his disciples, revealing esoteric teachings about the soul, suffering, and spiritual ascension. These texts, and many others from the Nag Hammadi library, offer a rich panorama of the figure of the Aeonic Christ, unveiling the multiple facets of his divine nature and his redemptive mission.

The figure of Christ as Aeon, therefore, represents a deep and mystical dimension of the Christian faith, which resonates with the human search for meaning, transcendence, and spiritual liberation. By contemplating Christ as an emanation of the Supreme Divinity, a being of light and wisdom who descended to the world to reveal Gnosis and guide humanity back to its divine origin, we can expand our understanding of the Christian message and enrich our own spiritual journey. Christ as Aeon invites us to look beyond the outward forms of religion, to seek the direct experience of spiritual truth, and to follow the path of Gnosis, the knowledge that liberates and transforms the human soul.

The exploration of the figure of the Aeonic Christ is an invitation to rediscover the depth and richness of esoteric Christianity and to experience the redemptive presence of the Aeon Christ in our own spiritual journey.

# Chapter 10
# The Holy Spirit, the Feminine Aeon

The Holy Spirit, understood as a feminine Aeon within the scope of Esoteric Christianity and the Gnostic tradition, reveals a deeply integrative facet of divinity, where the feminine principle—creative, nurturing, and inspiring—intertwines with the cosmic and spiritual structure of the universe. Her emanation directly from the divine fullness, the Pleroma, is not an isolated or secondary event, but an essential expression of the very fullness of the Supreme Monad, which, upon manifesting, reveals itself in both masculine and feminine polarities, unifying them in a cosmic dance of creation and revelation. This feminine Aeon is not merely a passive force of reception, but an active presence, radiating spiritual life and regenerative power, whose action takes place both in the higher planes of existence and in the intimate processes of awakening and inner evolution of the human soul. It is she who breathes the divine spark into the heart of each being, animating it with the breath of spiritual life and with the deep longing to return to its luminous origin.

Within the Pleroma, the function of the feminine Holy Spirit transcends mere sustenance of the cosmic order and reaches the level of direct divine inspiration.

She acts as a cosmic weaver, interlacing threads of wisdom and love in each spiritual emanation, ensuring that the divine essence remains alive in each Aeon, in each particle of light, and in each spark imprisoned in the veils of matter. Unlike more rigid conceptions that limit her to an impersonal force or a theological abstraction, this feminine view of the Holy Spirit presents her as a living, intimate, and welcoming presence, who participates directly in the journey of each soul, nurturing it with inspiration, intuition, and creative power. Her action is not authoritarian or directive, but subtle and loving, manifesting itself in deep perceptions, inner whispers, and flashes of spontaneous wisdom that lead the soul to the recognition of its true nature and to the conscious search for union with the divine.

As she descends from the higher spheres of the Pleroma to accompany the trajectory of fallen Sophia and all the souls who share her condition of spiritual exile, the feminine Holy Spirit takes on the role of invisible guide and inspiring breath that leads humanity to the awakening of Gnosis. This divine inspiration is not limited to isolated mystical events, but permeates all aspects of existence—from the creative capacity expressed in art and word to the intuitive flame that reveals hidden truths and guides crucial spiritual decisions. This feminine action of divinity rescues the sacredness of intuition and inner wisdom, recognizing that the spiritual quest is not merely an intellectual or doctrinal process, but a deep dive into the womb of the soul, where the voice of the Holy Spirit resonates as an echo of the Monad's own voice. Thus, recognizing the Holy Spirit as a feminine Aeon not only enriches Gnostic cosmology and Esoteric Christianity, but also reintegrates the sacred feminine into Western spirituality, restoring its essential role as guardian of spiritual life, intuitive knowledge, and the loving reconnection between the soul and its divine origin.

The interpretation of the Holy Spirit as a feminine Aeon is not universal within Gnosticism, but finds echoes in various traditions and texts, particularly those that emphasize the divine feminine principle and the figure of Sophia. In these contexts, the Holy Spirit is not merely the third person of the Trinity, but rather a specific manifestation of the Aeon Sophia, or even a distinct feminine Aeon, but intimately related to Sophia. This perspective does not seek to deny the Trinity, but rather to expand its understanding, revealing the presence and action of the divine feminine within the very essence of the Trinity.

The nature of the Holy Spirit, the feminine Aeon, is intrinsically linked to life, creation, and inspiration. She is seen as the vital force that animates the cosmos, the divine energy that permeates all living things and sustains existence. Just as Sophia is associated with divine wisdom, the Holy Spirit, the feminine Aeon, is linked to the creative and generative force of the Supreme Divinity, the power that gives rise to new forms and constantly renews life in the universe. This vital force is not only biological, but also spiritual, encompassing the energy that drives the growth of the soul, the awakening of consciousness, and the search for union with the divine.

The Holy Spirit, the feminine Aeon, is also understood as the source of divine inspiration, the power that illuminates the mind, ignites the heart, and awakens intuition. She is the inner voice that guides the spiritual seeker on the path of Gnosis, the force that impels the search for truth and self-knowledge. The inspiration of the Holy Spirit is not limited to moments of mystical revelation or religious ecstasy, but also manifests itself in artistic creativity, the capacity to love, the pursuit of justice, and in all forms of expression of the human soul that transcend mere materiality.

The association of the Holy Spirit with the divine feminine resonates with ancestral archetypes present in various cultures and religions throughout human history. The figure of the Mother Goddess, of the generating force of nature, of feminine wisdom, and of vital energy has always occupied a central place in the human imaginary, representing the source of life, nourishment, and inspiration. Interpreting the Holy Spirit as a feminine Aeon allows us to rescue and reintegrate these archetypes within Christianity, enriching its symbolism and expanding its ability to resonate with the human experience in its totality.

The relationship of the Holy Spirit, the feminine Aeon, with other Aeons, and in particular with the Supreme Divinity and the Aeon Christ, is a complex and multifaceted theme. In some Gnostic perspectives, the Holy Spirit is seen as the divine consort of the Monad, her feminine counterpart who complements the primordial unity. In this view, the Monad represents the divine masculine principle, transcendent and unknowable, while the Holy Spirit represents the divine feminine principle, immanent and manifesting. The union of the Monad and the Holy Spirit generates the fullness of the Pleroma and gives rise to the emanation of the other Aeons.

In other interpretations, the Holy Spirit, the feminine Aeon, is associated more specifically with the Aeon Christ, forming a syzygy or divine union that represents the manifestation of love and wisdom in the spiritual realm and the material world. In this perspective, Christ is the revealer of Gnosis and the guide to redemption, while the Holy Spirit is the force that inspires, animates, and empowers those who seek the path of Gnosis. The union of Christ and the Holy Spirit reflects the complementarity between the masculine principle of revelation and the feminine principle of inspiration and life.

It is important to note that the interpretation of the Holy Spirit as a feminine Aeon does not imply a denial of the masculinity of God the Father or the masculine role of Christ. It is an expansion of the understanding of the divine, which recognizes the presence and importance of both the masculine principle and the feminine principle in the Supreme Divinity. The Trinity, in this perspective, can be seen as an expression of the unity and diversity of the divine, encompassing both masculine and feminine polarities, and transcending the limitations of an exclusively masculine language and symbolism.

Spiritual practice that is inspired by the understanding of the Holy Spirit as a feminine Aeon can include various forms of devotion, meditation, and contemplation. Invoking the feminine Holy Spirit as a source of life and inspiration can strengthen the connection with the vital and creative energy of the universe, awaken intuition and inner wisdom, and nourish the soul with divine power. Meditation on the luminous and radiant nature of the feminine Holy Spirit can expand consciousness and open channels of communication with the higher spiritual dimensions of reality. Prayer and contemplation directed to the feminine Holy Spirit can generate a feeling of welcome, nourishment, and divine inspiration, strengthening faith and propelling the spiritual journey.

The exploration of the Holy Spirit as a feminine Aeon offers a rich and transformative perspective on the nature of the divine and spiritual experience. By rescuing the divine feminine principle and reintegrating it into esoteric Christian theology, this interpretation paves the way for a more balanced, inclusive, and resonant spirituality with the totality of human experience. The Holy Spirit, the feminine Aeon, invites us to recognize the vital and inspiring force that resides within us and throughout the universe, to awaken our intuition and inner wisdom, and to walk the path of Gnosis with the strength and inspiration of the divine feminine. Contemplation of the Holy Spirit as a feminine Aeon can profoundly enrich our spiritual journey, leading us to a deeper understanding of the divine mystery and a fuller experience of God's presence in our lives.

# Chapter 11
# Creation of the Material World

The emergence of the material world, in the context of Gnostic cosmology, reveals a profound unfolding of the divine order and its consequences on the plane of sensible existence. Unlike traditional creation narratives, which often associate the origin of the cosmos with an act of perfect will and wisdom on the part of a transcendent and benevolent God, the Gnostic view presents a conception in which the physical world is born from a disturbing event, marked by deviation, ignorance, and estrangement from the divine fullness. Material reality, with all its density, duality, and suffering, does not represent a direct creation of the Supreme Source, the Monad or the One, but rather the result of the action of a derived entity, the Demiurge, whose own emergence is rooted in a cosmic and spiritual rupture. This tangible universe is, therefore, a secondary and distorted reality, lacking the true light and harmony proper to the Pleroma—the spiritual region from which the Aeons emanate, luminous beings and aspects of the primordial divinity itself.

The key to understanding this process lies in the fall of the Aeon Sophia, a fundamental event in Gnostic mythology, in which the intense desire to know and reach the source of the divine, without proper mediation, leads to the generation of an imperfect emanation. This emanation, detached from the harmonious order of the Pleroma, gives rise to an entity that, although endowed with creative power, is devoid of full gnosis, that is, of the profound knowledge of the true divine and cosmic nature. This entity is the Demiurge, whose ignorance leads him to believe that he himself is the origin and apex of existence, thus becoming a blind artificer who molds the material world from his limitation and arrogance. His creation, therefore, reflects the incompleteness of his own essence: a fragmented world, marked by irreconcilable polarities—light and darkness, spirit and matter, suffering and the search for meaning. This view does not deny that creation possesses elements of order and beauty, but these elements are diluted vestiges of the original light, which remain even after the fall and separation from the Pleroma.

The role of the Aeons, in this context, is not that of passive or distant agents in relation to the material world, but rather of active powers that seek, in various ways, to re-establish the connection between the imprisoned spirit and its transcendent origin. Even with the creation of the physical world being attributed to the Demiurge and the Archons, the Aeons maintain their presence and influence, serving as sources of spiritual inspiration and revelation of Gnosis. The Gnostic revelation is, in itself, an intervention of the Aeons, whose light penetrates the layers of illusion erected by the Demiurge and his assistants, providing the human soul with the possibility of remembering its true origin and awakening to its divine essence. Thus, the creation of the material world is not just an error or cosmic accident, but a spiritual battlefield in which luminous and dark forces dispute the fate of the divine sparks imprisoned in the flesh. Gnostic cosmology, therefore, does not propose a simplistic rejection of matter, but a view in which the physical world is a territory of challenge and learning, where spiritual ascension and the recovery of lost unity only become possible through the recognition of the true origin and the liberation from the veil of ignorance imposed by the demiurgic creation.

The relationship between the Aeons and the Demiurge is not one of harmonious collaboration, but rather of complex interaction, marked by a certain tension and misunderstanding. While the Aeons inhabit the Pleroma, the realm of light, truth, and perfection, the Demiurge arises from a disturbance or deviation within this realm, often associated with the fall of the Aeon Sophia. The Demiurge is not a direct emanation of the Monad, but rather an entity generated from an inferior or imperfect emanation, lacking the full knowledge and light of the Supreme Divinity. This differentiated origin gives the Demiurge a nature distinct from the Aeons, characterized by a certain ignorance, arrogance, and limitation in relation to the true divine reality.

The Demiurge's role in the creation of the material world is central to Gnostic cosmology. It is to him that the formation of the physical cosmos is attributed, with its heavens, earth, stars, and all the creatures that inhabit it. However, the Demiurge's creation is not seen as an act of kindness or divine wisdom, but rather as a consequence of his ignorance and his pretense of being the one and true God. The Demiurge, unaware of the existence of the Supreme Divinity and the Pleroma, believes himself to be the supreme being and proclaims himself as such, creating the material world as a kind of imperfect imitation of the divine realm, but without the true light and perfection of the Pleroma.

The creation of the material world by the Demiurge is described as a process of inverted or distorted emanation, in contrast to the luminous and ascending emanation of the Aeons from the Monad. The Demiurge, in his ignorance, emanates a series of inferior spiritual beings, the Archons, who assist him in the creation and governance of the material world. These Archons, like the Demiurge, are characterized by darkness, illusion, and hostility towards humanity and the pursuit of Gnosis. They act as oppressive forces, seeking to keep humanity imprisoned in the ignorance and suffering of the material world, preventing spiritual awakening and the return to the Pleroma.

The material world created by the Demiurge, therefore, reflects the imperfection and ignorance of its creator. It is a world marked by duality, conflict, change, and mortality. The light of the Pleroma, although present in a tenuous and dispersed form, is obscured by the density of matter and the influence of the Archons. Suffering, pain, disease, and death are seen as inherent characteristics of the material condition, reflections of the imperfection of the demiurgic creation and the distance of the material world from divine fullness.

Within this material world, humanity occupies a unique and paradoxical position. The human being is conceived as possessing a dual nature: a material body, created by the Demiurge and subject to the laws of the material world, and a divine spark, the spirit or soul, which comes from the Pleroma and is imprisoned in matter. This divine spark, the pneuma, represents the true essence of the human being, his connection with the spiritual world, and his ability to achieve Gnosis and redemption. The Demiurge, unaware of the divine origin of the human spiritual spark, seeks to keep it imprisoned in matter, preventing its awakening and its return to the Pleroma.

The relationship between the Aeons and the creation of the material world is not limited to the action of the Demiurge. Although the Demiurge is the creator of the physical world, the Aeons play an important role in the cosmic economy, seeking to mitigate the effects of demiurgic ignorance and offer humanity the possibility of redemption. The Aeon Christ, in particular, descends into the material world with the mission of revealing Gnosis and awakening the sleeping souls, offering the path of spiritual liberation and the return to the Pleroma. Other Aeons also act as guides and helpers, inspiring spiritual seekers, protecting them from the negative influences of the Archons, and leading them on the path of Gnosis.

The action of the Aeons in the material world can be seen as an attempt to restore the divine order and to repair the damage caused by the imperfect creation of the Demiurge. The Aeons do not seek to destroy the material world, but rather to transform it, illuminating it with the light of Gnosis and awakening the divine spark imprisoned in matter. Redemption, from the Gnostic perspective, does not imply escape or denial of the material world, but rather the transformation of human consciousness and the elevation of the spirit above the limitations of matter.

It is important to note that the Gnostic view of the creation of the material world and the role of the Demiurge is not an absolute condemnation of matter or the physical world. Although the material world is seen as imperfect and marked by suffering, it is also recognized as a field of experience and learning for the human soul. The Gnostic spiritual journey is not about escaping the material world, but rather about awakening to the spiritual reality within the material world, discovering the inner divine spark, and walking the path of Gnosis amidst the illusions and challenges of earthly existence.

The figure of the Demiurge, in his complexity and ambiguity, represents a challenge to the traditional view of a benevolent and omnipotent creator God. Gnostic cosmology, by attributing the creation of the material world to an imperfect and ignorant entity, raises profound questions about the nature of evil, suffering, and human freedom. The Gnostic view does not offer easy or simplistic answers, but rather invites a deep reflection on the human condition and the search for transcendent meaning in a world marked by imperfection and duality.

The exploration of the relationship between the Aeons and the creation of the material world, with the central role of the Demiurge, allows us to delve into one of the most challenging and intriguing aspects of Gnostic cosmology. Understanding the Gnostic view of the origin of the world and the nature of the Demiurge is fundamental to grasping the message of redemption and the path of Gnosis proposed by esoteric Christianity. The interaction between the Aeons and the Demiurge, in its complexity and tension, reflects the dynamics of the Gnostic universe, a field of spiritual forces in constant movement and transformation, where the search for light and truth unfolds amidst the shadows of ignorance and illusion.

# Chapter 12
# Functions of the Aeons

The Aeons, in their luminous and transcendent nature, emerge from the Pleroma as living expressions of the divine fullness, manifesting essential aspects of the Supreme Being. They not only reflect the totality of the Original Source, but also play an active role in sustaining the cosmic order and transmitting Gnosis, the knowledge that liberates. Distinct in their qualities and functions, the Aeons operate as links between the absolute realm of spirit and the fragmented reality of matter, serving as spiritual guides and as archetypes of truth and awakening. Their existence is not limited to contemplation of the divine light; on the contrary, they are dynamic agents of creation, preservation, and restoration of cosmic harmony. At the heart of their activity is the commitment to ensure the continuity of the primordial unity and to offer humanity the means to transcend the ignorance imposed by the material world.

The role of the Aeons transcends the mere organization of the Pleroma, as their influence extends to the lower cosmos, where matter and duality reign. Although the physical world was shaped by the Demiurge, a limited being distanced from supreme wisdom, the presence of the Aeons resonates as a subtle call to the truth hidden beneath the layers of illusion. They operate as messengers of the Pleroma, channeling spiritual influxes that penetrate the demiurgic creation, offering guidance to those who seek self-knowledge and liberation. Their emanations reach humanity through mystical revelations, philosophical inspirations, and transformative experiences, allowing individuals to awaken to their true nature. Thus, the Aeons fulfill a pedagogical function, assisting in the soul's journey back to its divine origin, leading it through a process of purification and illumination. Each act of Gnosis is a reflection of Aeonic influence, a glimpse of the primordial light that still shines, even amidst the darkness of material existence.

The action of the Aeons in human redemption reveals their compassion and direct involvement in the trajectory of souls exiled in the lower world. The Aeon Christ, for example, represents the purest manifestation of divine love by descending into the material realm to transmit saving knowledge. His mission is not only to teach, but to remind humanity of its true essence, awakening it from the lethargy imposed by the forces of forgetfulness. Likewise, Sophia, whose tragic journey reflects the fall and the search for return to the Pleroma, acts as an archetype of the soul in its journey of reunion with the light. Her repentance and desire for restoration resonate in human experience, becoming a model for those who yearn for reintegration with the divine. The presence of the Aeons, therefore, is not limited to the celestial realm; they permeate all dimensions of existence, offering paths to transcendence and reaffirming that, despite the illusory separation, the connection with the Pleroma has never been completely lost.

One of the primary functions of the Aeons is cosmic organization. Within the Pleroma, the Aeons act as harmonizing and balancing forces, maintaining divine order and ensuring the cohesion and stability of the spiritual realm. Each Aeon, with its specific attributes and functions, contributes to the complex web of relationships and interconnections that characterize the Pleroma. The Aeonic hierarchy, with its families, orders, and relationships, reflects the intrinsic order of the spiritual cosmos, a dynamic and fluid, yet fundamentally harmonious, organization. The Aeons, in their joint action, ensure that divine energy flows freely through the Pleroma, sustaining life and consciousness at all levels of the spiritual realm. They act as gears in a perfect cosmic machine, each playing its role with precision and in synchrony with the others, for the harmonious functioning of the whole.

The organizing function of the Aeons is not limited to the Pleroma, extending also, in an indirect and mediated way, to the material world. Although the material world is the creation of the imperfect Demiurge, the Aeons exert a subtle and beneficial influence on it, seeking to contain the chaos and imperfection inherent in the demiurgic creation. Through their emanations and their spiritual influence, the Aeons seek to imprint a certain order and harmony on the material world, guiding natural processes, regulating cosmic cycles, and discreetly influencing the course of earthly events. This influence of the Aeons on the material world is not an authoritarian imposition, but rather a subtle persuasion, a call to order and harmony that resonates in the depths of material reality.

In addition to cosmic organization, the Aeons also play a fundamental role in the evolution of consciousness. In the Gnostic view, human consciousness, imprisoned in matter and obscured by ignorance, has the potential to awaken to its true spiritual nature and to the divine reality. The Aeons act as agents of awakening, inspiring spiritual seekers, stimulating the search for truth, and offering the necessary assistance for the soul's journey towards Gnosis. They radiate wisdom and discernment, illuminating the path of Gnosis and removing the obstacles that stand between the human soul and its union with the divine. This evolutionary function of the Aeons manifests itself in various forms, from artistic and philosophical inspiration to mystical revelation and the direct experience of spiritual truth.

The evolution of consciousness, in the Gnostic perspective, is not a linear and automatic process, but rather a complex and challenging journey, which requires effort, discernment, and perseverance. The Aeons do not force the evolution of consciousness, but rather offer the necessary help and guidance to those who choose to tread the path of Gnosis. The response to the inspiration and call of the Aeons depends on the free will and inner disposition of each individual. The evolution of consciousness is, therefore, a cooperative process, a dance between human initiative and divine grace, between individual effort and the assistance of the Aeons.

The redemptive function of the Aeons is perhaps the most significant and the most directly related to the human condition. In Gnostic cosmology, humanity finds itself in a state of spiritual exile, imprisoned in matter and obscured by ignorance. Redemption, in this context, does not primarily refer to the remission of sins or salvation from eternal damnation, but rather to liberation from ignorance, the awakening of spiritual consciousness, and the return to the fullness of the Pleroma. The Aeons, moved by compassion and divine love, act as agents of redemption, offering humanity the possibility of escaping the captivity of matter and achieving union with the Supreme Divinity.

The Aeon Christ, in particular, assumes a central role in human redemption. Descending from the Pleroma to the material world, Christ reveals Gnosis, the saving knowledge that liberates from ignorance and illusion. He offers a path of inner transformation, a method of self-knowledge and spiritual awakening that leads to redemption and return to the divine origin. The message of Christ, in the Gnostic perspective, is a message of liberation, hope, and radical transformation of consciousness. Christ not only teaches the path of redemption, but also offers his assistance and spiritual presence to those who dedicate themselves to following it. He is the Gnostic savior, the redeemer who guides awakened souls back to the Pleroma.

The redemptive function of the Aeons is not limited to the figure of Christ. Other Aeons also act as helpers in human redemption, offering different forms of spiritual assistance and guidance. Sophia, the Divine Wisdom, seeks to restore cosmic order and rescue the divine sparks imprisoned in matter. The feminine Holy Spirit Aeon inspires, animates, and empowers spiritual seekers, strengthening their faith and propelling their inner journey. Various other Aeons act as guides, protectors, and mentors, offering wisdom, discernment, and strength to those who seek Gnosis and redemption.

The action of the Aeons in human redemption is not a magical or automatic process, but rather a path of inner transformation that requires effort, dedication, and perseverance. Gnosis is not a free gift or a divine gift granted without effort, but rather the fruit of a sincere search and constant spiritual practice. The Aeons offer the necessary help and guidance, but the final responsibility for the spiritual journey and the pursuit of redemption lies with each individual. Gnostic redemption is, therefore, an active and participatory process, a collaboration between divine grace and human free will, between the assistance of the Aeons and individual effort.

The functions of the Aeons, encompassing cosmic organization, the evolution of consciousness, and human redemption, reveal the depth and complexity of the Gnostic vision of the universe and humanity's role within it. The Aeons, as divine forces and cosmic intelligences, act constantly and dynamically to maintain cosmic order, promote spiritual evolution, and offer the possibility of redemption. Understanding the functions of the Aeons is fundamental to grasping the central message of esoteric Christianity and to treading the path of Gnosis in search of union with the divine. The action of the Aeons invites us to awaken to our true spiritual nature, to seek saving knowledge, and to collaborate with the divine forces in the restoration of cosmic harmony and the realization of our ultimate destiny in the Pleroma.

# Chapter 13
# Aeons and Time

In the Pleroma, the luminous and immaterial dwelling where the Aeons reside, time is not perceived as a continuous line of chained events, but rather as a full, immutable, and comprehensive dimension, where past, present, and future do not exist as separate categories. The existence of the Aeons occurs in a living eternity, where all aspects of being coexist in a simultaneous and indivisible totality. This eternity is not a static suspension, but an incessant vibration of potentialities that manifest without rupture or succession, so that each Aeon contains within itself the fullness of its essence in perfect harmony with all others. The Pleroma, by its very timeless nature, does not know the fragmentation of experience, an essential characteristic of the human condition in the lower world. The eternity lived by the Aeons is a continuous and absolute presence, where there is no weight of expectation of the future or the melancholic echo of the lost past, but only a total presence, where each instant, if it can be so called, summarizes and manifests the totality of the divine being.

This contrast between Aeonic eternity and the linear temporality of the material world constitutes a fundamental key to understanding the existential drama of the human soul, imprisoned in a universe governed by the relentless succession of events and the irreversibility of time. In the lower cosmos, shaped by ignorance and separation, time imposes itself as a force of attrition and limitation, subjecting everything to impermanence, to continuous flux, and to the impossibility of retaining any instant. Time, in the world created by the Demiurge, is not a simple measure of change, but a manifestation of the very incompleteness of material existence, marked by ruptures, ends, and beginnings, in absolute contrast to the continuous fullness of the Pleroma. This temporal linearity, which defines the common human experience, is not only an external condition imposed by the material environment, but an internal structure of the incarnated consciousness itself, which has learned to think and feel from the division between past, present, and future, becoming a prisoner of this fragmented logic.

Gnosis, as revelation and direct experience of divine truth, breaks this veil of temporality and offers the soul the possibility of rediscovering within itself the presence of eternity hidden under the layers of linear perception. The Gnostic spiritual journey is, to a large extent, a process of deconstructing this tyranny of psychological and existential time, allowing the seeker to access a dimension of consciousness where eternity is not a distant promise, but a reality already present, pulsating at the core of being itself. This opening to Aeonic eternity, however, does not require the denial of earthly life or the flight from chronological time; on the contrary, it allows linear time to be re-signified, recognized as a surface where eternity insinuates itself in brief glimpses, in moments of intuition and revelation. Every fully lived moment, every flash of spiritual clarity, every experience of deep integration between body, mind, and spirit, becomes a door to this underlying eternity. The soul that awakens to this simultaneous reality is able to inhabit time without getting lost in it, recognizing the illusory character of its apparent linearity and perceiving, under the incessant flow of events, the constant presence of immutable fullness, of which the Aeons are guardians and living manifestations.

In the realm of the Pleroma, where the Aeons reside, time takes on a quality radically different from that which we experience in the material world. For the Aeons, time does not manifest as a linear progression of past, present, and future, but rather as a present eternity, a state of timeless being that encompasses all existence in a single instant. In this context, time is not a limiting or conditioning factor, but rather a transcended dimension, an overcoming of the succession and change that characterize the temporal reality of the material world. Aeonic eternity should not be confused with a mere indefinite extension of linear time, but rather with a qualitatively different mode of existence, where temporality, as we understand it, ceases to have validity.

The eternity of the Aeons does not imply stagnation or immobility, but rather a dynamic and incessant fullness. In the Pleroma, time is not a river that flows in a linear direction, but rather a vast and deep ocean, where all waters are interconnected and present simultaneously. The Aeons, immersed in this present eternity, experience the totality of existence in a single now, transcending the fragmentation and temporal succession that limit human perception in the material world. This eternity is not empty or monotonous, but rather full of life, consciousness, and divine activity. The Aeons, in their present eternity, participate in the incessant dynamics of the Pleroma, contributing to the cosmic order and to the manifestation of divine will.

In contrast to Aeonic eternity, human reality in the material world unfolds under the dominion of linear time. Linear time, as we perceive and experience it, is characterized by the sequence of events, by the progression from the past to the future through the present, and by the irreversibility of the temporal flow. In this temporal mode, the past is gone, the future has not yet arrived, and the present continually fades away, giving way to the next instant. Linear time imposes limits on human existence, marking the beginning and end of life, the change and impermanence of all things, and the inevitability of aging and death.

The linear perception of time is intrinsically linked to our experience in the material world, conditioned by corporeality, sensoriality, and the rational mind. Our senses present us with a world in constant flux, where things are born, grow, transform, and disappear. Our rational mind, in turn, organizes experience into temporal categories, establishing cause-and-effect relationships, projecting the future from the past, and constructing a linear narrative of our own existence and the history of the world. Linear time thus becomes a filter through which we perceive and interpret material reality, shaping our consciousness and our experience of the world.

The search for Gnosis, in the context of esoteric Christianity, represents a path to transcend the limitations of linear time and to glimpse Aeonic eternity. Gnosis, as intuitive and transformative knowledge of spiritual truth, offers the human soul the possibility of breaking the bonds of linear temporal perception and accessing a dimension of consciousness that transcends time and space. Through the practice of meditation, contemplation, and interiorization, the seeker of Gnosis can silence the rational mind, quiet the incessant flow of thoughts and temporal concerns, and open oneself to the experience of the present eternity that resides in the depths of being.

Gnosis, as an experience of temporal transcendence, does not imply escaping linear time or denying the reality of earthly existence. On the contrary, the Gnostic quest seeks to integrate the experience of eternity into daily life, to live in linear time with the awareness of present eternity. By glimpsing the eternity of the Aeons, the seeker of Gnosis can relativize the importance of linear time, recognizing its transitory and illusory nature in comparison with the eternal and immutable reality of the Pleroma. This relativized perspective of linear time does not lead to negligence or contempt for earthly life, but rather to a fuller and more conscious experience of the present, to a valuation of the fleeting instant, and to a deeper understanding of the ephemeral nature of material existence.

Understanding the timeless nature of the Aeons and our own immersion in linear time can transform our perspective on life and spirituality. Recognizing that eternity is not a distant future or an inaccessible realm, but rather a dimension present and active in our own being, can inspire a deeper search for mystical experience and union with the divine. Spiritual practice, in this context, becomes a path to awaken to present eternity, to cultivate timeless consciousness, and to live in the linear world with the wisdom and serenity that emanate from the understanding of eternity.

Symbolically, the linear nature of time can be represented by a straight line, which extends infinitely in two directions, representing the past and the future. This straight line symbolizes the sequence, progression, and irreversibility of linear time, its fleeting and transitory nature. In contrast, Aeonic eternity can be symbolized by a circle, a geometric figure that has no beginning or end, that closes upon itself, representing totality, fullness, and present eternity. The circle symbolizes the timeless and cyclical nature of spiritual reality, its immutability, and its constant presence in all moments. The image of the circle as a symbol of Aeonic eternity can assist in meditation and contemplation, inspiring the soul to transcend the linearity of time and to seek union with the timeless divine.

The exploration of the relationship between the Aeons and time invites us to rethink our perception of reality and to expand our understanding of the nature of time. Recognizing the existence of a present eternity, inhabited by the Aeons and accessible through Gnosis, can transform our experience of linear time, giving it a new meaning and a new depth. The Gnostic spiritual journey, in its quest for union with the timeless divine, represents a path to transcend the limitations of earthly existence and to glimpse the eternity that resides in the heart of being. The contemplation of Aeonic eternity can profoundly enrich our lives, inspiring us to live in the present with more fullness, awareness, and serenity, and to tread the path of Gnosis in search of union with the Supreme Divinity, which transcends time and encompasses all eternity.

# Chapter 14
# Aeonic Variations

The diversity of Gnostic systems manifests itself in a particularly rich and revealing way in how different schools conceived, named, and organized the Aeons, spiritual entities that inhabit the Pleroma and personify fundamental aspects of the divine fullness. This plurality of approaches is not the result of contradiction or arbitrary fragmentation, but rather an expression of the dynamic and fluid nature of Gnostic thought itself, which adapts to the traditions, philosophical currents, and spiritual needs of each Gnostic community. Thus, instead of a fixed and uniform pantheon, what is observed is a multiplicity of Aeonic constellations, where each Gnostic system shapes its own celestial architecture, reflecting different understandings of the origin, structure, and purpose of the spiritual cosmos. This variation, far from weakening the unity of Gnostic thought, reveals its ability to dialogue with different cultures and to continuously reinterpret its visions of the divine, the soul, and the path of redemption.

In Gnostic systems linked to the Valentinian tradition, the Aeons are presented in a detailed and highly ordered manner, forming a chain of emanations that extend from the unfathomable depth of the Supreme

Father to the outer limits of the Pleroma. Each Aeon is conceived as a complementary manifestation of another, configuring pairs or syzygies that symbolize the balance between masculine and feminine principles at the heart of divine reality. This dynastic and relational conception emphasizes the harmony and interdependence of all emanations, highlighting the progressive manifestation of divinity through a process of self-knowledge and self-expression. In contrast, in Sethianism, the Aeonic structure is less hierarchical and more centered on a primordial triad—Father, Mother, and Son—where Barbelo, the Divine Mother, assumes a central role as cosmic matrix and source of all subsequent emanations. In this context, Sethian Aeons are less numerous and less rigidly organized, reflecting a more mythical and less systematic conception of spiritual reality, in which the mystery of divine emanation is prioritized over the construction of a meticulous genealogical order.

These variations are not limited to the quantity or internal organization of the Aeons, but are also reflected in the attributes, functions, and symbolism associated with them. In Valentinian systems, each Aeon represents a specific divine quality, such as Truth, Grace, Intelligence, or Union, composing a kind of sacred vocabulary that expresses the totality of the spiritual powers of the Pleroma. In Sethianism, on the other hand, Aeons often assume names and functions linked to cosmic and mythological archetypes, such as the Hidden One (Kalyptos) or the Self-Generated (Autogenes), suggesting a cosmology in which Aeons play active roles in the cosmic drama of the fall and redemption.

This conceptual plasticity demonstrates how Gnostic thought was able to continuously reinterpret and resignify the function of the Aeons, adapting them to the symbolic and spiritual needs of different communities. This fluidity allowed the concept of Aeons to serve as a bridge between individual mystical experience and collective metaphysical speculation, providing a symbolic language capable of expressing both the most abstract theological visions and the most intimate spiritual experiences.

Thus, the Aeonic diversity in Gnostic systems does not represent an obstacle to understanding the doctrine, but rather a testimony to its creative vitality and its openness to multiple perspectives and interpretations. Each Gnostic school, by reorganizing and renaming the Aeons, is not only composing a new cosmic map, but also offering a specific key to understanding the drama of the human soul in its exile and its search for return to the divine. The variation of the Aeons is, therefore, a direct expression of the Gnostic view that the divine is inexhaustible and that each attempt to name it or describe its emanations is only a partial facet of a greater truth, always open to new revelations and new paths of understanding. To understand this Aeonic plurality is to recognize Gnostic thought as a fertile field of dialogue between tradition and innovation, between myth and philosophy, between personal experience and cosmic vision, where the divine reveals itself not as a single and immutable truth, but as an infinite possibility of emanation and return.

Within the Gnostic panorama, the Valentinian system, originating from the teachings of Valentinus of Alexandria in the 2nd century AD, stands out for its elaborate and refined Aeonic cosmology. Valentinus and his followers developed a complex system of divine emanations, detailing the genealogy and relationships between the Aeons in a meticulous manner. In the Valentinian system, the Pleroma is structured as a dynastic hierarchy, with pairs of Aeons (syzygies) emanating from each other in a descending progression, from the primordial principles to the most distant manifestations of the Supreme Divinity.

At the apex of the Valentinian hierarchy resides the first syzygy, composed of the Ineffable Father or Depth (Bythos) and Thought (Ennoia or Sige, Silence). Bythos represents the primordial, transcendent, and unknowable principle of the Supreme Divinity, while Ennoia is his primordial thought or consciousness, the feminine principle that complements him. From this first syzygy emanates the second, constituted by Mind (Nous or Monogenes, Only-Begotten) and Truth (Aletheia). Nous represents divine intelligence, the ability to know and discern, while Aletheia is the primordial truth, the perfect knowledge of divine reality.

From the syzygy of Nous and Aletheia, other syzygies emanate, each manifesting specific attributes and functions within the Pleroma. These emanations continue in geometric progression, forming a complex hierarchy of thirty Aeons (in some versions, thirty-two), arranged in various orders and groupings. Among the best-known Valentinian Aeons are Word (Logos) and

Life (Zoe), Man (Anthropos) and Church (Ecclesia), Christ and Holy Spirit, Faith (Pistis) and Hope (Elpis), Charity (Agape) and Perfection (Teleiosis), among many others. Each Valentinian Aeon personifies a divine quality, an aspect of the perfection and fullness of the Pleroma, contributing to the richness and complexity of the spiritual realm.

In contrast to the elaborate Valentinian hierarchy, the Sethian system, originating from Gnostic groups that claimed descent from Seth, the third son of Adam, presents an Aeonic cosmology with distinct characteristics. Sethianism, whose texts were found at Nag Hammadi, emphasizes the figure of Seth as a spiritual ancestor of the Gnostic lineage and presents a cosmogony that differs in some respects from the Valentinian view. Although the concept of Aeons is also present in Sethianism, the hierarchical organization and nomenclature of these spiritual beings differ significantly.

In the Sethian system, the Supreme Divinity is often designated as the Invisible and Ineffable Spirit, or simply the Father. From this primordial source emanates a triad of primordial beings: the Father, the Mother, and the Son. The Mother, in Sethianism, assumes a prominent role, often identified as Barbelo, a primordial feminine Aeon associated with divine wisdom and creative power. Barbelo is seen as the first emanation of the Father, his perfect image and the feminine principle that complements him. The Son, in the Sethian triad, is generally identified with Autogenes (Self-Generated) or

Christ, representing the manifestation of divine intelligence and light in the Pleroma.

From this primordial Sethian triad, other generations of Aeons emanate, forming a hierarchy less elaborate and less dynastic than the Valentinian one. The Sethian system tends to emphasize the unity and transcendence of the Supreme Divinity, with a smaller number of Aeons and less emphasis on genealogy and family relationships between them. Some prominent Sethian Aeons include Kalyptos (The Hidden One), Protophanes (First Manifestation), Triploprópros (Triply Providential), and many others, each with specific attributes and functions within the Sethian cosmology.

When comparing the Valentinian and Sethian Aeonic hierarchies, some notable similarities and differences emerge. Both systems share the fundamental belief in Aeons as emanations of the Supreme Divinity, inhabitants of the Pleroma, and intermediaries between the transcendent world and the material world. Both systems also recognize the existence of a hierarchy of spiritual beings, with different levels of proximity to the Supreme Divinity and different functions within the cosmic order. The presence of Aeons such as Christ and Sophia, although with different nuances of interpretation, is also a common feature of both systems.

However, the differences between the Valentinian and Sethian Aeonic hierarchies are also significant. The Valentinian system stands out for its elaboration and genealogical detail, with a greater number of Aeons organized in syzygies and complex hierarchies. Sethianism, on the other hand, presents a more simplified hierarchy, with a smaller number of Aeons and an emphasis on the primordial triad of Father-Mother-Son. The nomenclature of the Aeons also varies considerably between the two systems, reflecting different theological and cosmological emphases. While the Valentinian system tends to emphasize the gradual and hierarchical procession of divine emanation, Sethianism seems to prioritize the unity and transcendence of the Supreme Divinity and the primordial role of the Divine Mother, Barbelo.

The Aeonic variations in different Gnostic systems can be attributed to several factors, including different interpretations of scriptures, diverse philosophical influences, and the historical evolution of Gnostic thought over time. The different Gnostic communities, spread across various regions of the ancient world, developed their own interpretations and elaborations of the Aeonic cosmology, reflecting their cultural contexts, their theological concerns, and their specific spiritual experiences. Aeonic diversity, therefore, is a testimony to the richness and vitality of Gnostic thought, its ability to adapt and express itself in multiple forms, while preserving a common core of ideas and principles.

Beyond the Valentinian and Sethian systems, other Gnostic schools and currents also presented variations in their Aeonic hierarchies. The Basilidian system, for example, developed by Basilides of Alexandria in the 2nd century AD, proposed an Aeonic cosmology even more complex and elaborate than the Valentinian one, with an even greater number of Aeons and intricate hierarchies. Other Gnostic currents, such as Mandaeism and Manichaeism, although not fitting perfectly into the category of Christian Gnosticism, also developed cosmological systems with intermediate spiritual entities that can be compared, to some extent, to Gnostic Aeons.

The comparative view of Aeonic variations in different Gnostic systems allows us to appreciate the richness and diversity of Gnostic thought and its ability to generate multiple interpretations and elaborations of the spiritual cosmology. Recognizing these variations is essential to avoid overgeneralizations and to understand the complexity and nuance of the Gnostic legacy. Aeonic diversity does not weaken the central notion of Aeons as divine emanations, but rather enriches it, revealing the multiple facets and infinite possibilities of expression of the divine in the Gnostic universe. The exploration of Aeonic variations is, therefore, a path to a deeper and more complete understanding of Gnostic thought and its singular vision of spiritual reality.

# Chapter 15
# Criticisms of the Concept

Since its earliest formulations in Gnostic traditions, the concept of Aeons has aroused both fascination and resistance, especially when confronted with emerging Christian orthodoxy and its efforts to consolidate a unified and monotheistic theological vision. The Aeons, conceived as emanations of the Supreme Divinity and inhabitants of a sphere of spiritual fullness, presented a cosmological structure that challenged the simplicity and uniqueness of God, central foundations of the nascent Christian faith. While for the Gnostics the Aeons represented aspects of the divinity itself in its creative unfolding, for orthodox Christian thinkers this multiplicity of spiritual powers was readily interpreted as a veiled form of polytheism, an unacceptable fragmentation of divine unity. The very fact that the Pleroma was inhabited by hierarchical emanations polarized into male-female pairs was read as a rupture of divine simplicity, which, according to orthodox theology, did not require internal unfolding or complements to express its fullness and perfection.

Beyond the accusation of diluting divine unity, the concept of Aeons was criticized for implying a vision of creation and the cosmos radically different from the doctrine of creation *ex nihilo*. Instead of affirming a direct, free, and sovereign creative act, Gnostic cosmology postulated a process of successive emanations, where each Aeon, as it emerged, brought with it a slight degradation or distancing in relation to the original fullness. This cyclical and descending view of creation not only contrasted with the idea of a universe created as essentially good, but also introduced an ontological gradation that compromised the fundamental equality of all creatures before the Creator. The Church Fathers, especially Irenaeus of Lyon, fought against this notion by defending a direct and personal relationship between God and creation, without the need for divine intermediaries or spiritual hierarchies that filtered or limited the contact between Creator and creature. The existence of Aeons was, therefore, seen as an unnecessary and theologically dangerous complication, which distanced man from confidence in an accessible and immanent God, replacing this direct relationship with a network of powers and barriers that distanced the soul from its Creator.

If historically the concept of Aeons was rejected as heretical and incompatible with the orthodox Christian view, modern and contemporary thought, especially in the areas of depth psychology, philosophy of religion, and esoteric spirituality, has brought a symbolic and archetypal revaluation of these same Aeons. For thinkers like Carl Jung, the Aeons ceased to be just metaphysical entities and came to be understood as archetypal representations of fundamental psychic dynamics. In his investigations of alchemy and

Gnosticism, Jung saw in the Aeons symbolic personifications of the processes of individuation, where the psyche seeks to integrate and balance its internal polarities — masculine and feminine, conscious and unconscious, light and shadow. In this psychological key, the Aeons became mirrors of the internal structures of the human soul, symbolic maps of the search for wholeness and meaning, translating into mythological images the same processes that, in the field of analytical psychology, emerge as existential crises, identity transformations, and processes of self-knowledge.

This symbolic rescue of the concept of Aeons allowed that, even outside the original Gnostic context, these spiritual entities were reinterpreted as universal archetypes, present in multiple cultures and spiritual traditions. In contemporary esoteric movements and in the so-called New Age spirituality, the Aeons were reintroduced as cosmic intelligences, spiritual guides, or manifestations of divine qualities accessible to human consciousness through meditative practices, mystical visions, or invocation rituals. This modern appropriation not only made the concept more flexible, adapting it to different spiritual and philosophical languages, but also reinforced its relevance as a symbol of a spiritual reality that transcends dogmas and fixed religious systems. Thus, even the target of severe historical and theological criticisms, the concept of Aeons remains alive as a plastic and dynamic expression of the eternal human search to understand its divine origin, its existential fragmentation, and the path of return to the primordial source, whether it is described as Pleroma, Self, or Cosmic Consciousness.

The historical criticisms of the concept of Aeons originated mainly within orthodox Christianity, from the 2nd century AD, when the Church Fathers, such as Irenaeus of Lyon, Hippolytus of Rome, and Tertullian, dedicated themselves to refuting Gnostic doctrines considered heretical and deviant from the authentic Christian faith. These Christian polemicists, in their works combating Gnosis, directed forceful criticisms at the concept of Aeons, questioning its theological validity and its compatibility with the Gospel message. The orthodox criticisms of the Aeons focused on several crucial points of Gnostic cosmology.

One of the main points of orthodox criticism of the Aeons concerns their origin and their nature in relation to the Supreme Divinity. The Church Fathers argued that the emanation of the Aeons from the Monad, as described by the Gnostics, compromised the unity and simplicity of God, introducing a complex and potentially divisive hierarchy within the divine essence itself. For the orthodox, God is one and indivisible, the absolute creator of all things from nothing, and not a primordial source that emanates a series of intermediate spiritual beings. The emanation of the Aeons was seen as a form of disguised polytheism or as a dilution of divinity, incompatible with monotheistic faith and with the doctrine of creation *ex nihilo*.

Another relevant orthodox criticism of the Aeons refers to their role in the creation of the material world and the figure of the Demiurge. The Church Fathers rejected the Gnostic view of a material world created by an imperfect and ignorant entity of the true Supreme Divinity, arguing that God, being good and omnipotent, is the sole creator of the universe, including both the spiritual world and the material world. The Gnostic duality between a transcendent and good God and a creator and imperfect Demiurge was considered heretical, as it implied a division in divinity and a pessimistic view of creation, incompatible with divine goodness and providence. The identification of the Demiurge with the God of the Old Testament, present in some Gnostic strands, was also strongly criticized by the orthodox, who defended the unity and continuity between the God of the Old and New Testaments.

In addition to theological criticisms, the Church Fathers also questioned the validity of Gnostic sources, such as the Apocryphal Gospels and Gnostic texts in general, considered spurious, late, and devoid of apostolic authority. Gnostic texts were seen as works of heretical sects, intended to divert the faithful from the true Christian faith and to propagate false and misleading doctrines. The authority of the canonical scriptures, of the Old and New Testaments, was contrasted with the supposed falsehood and fragility of the Gnostic sources, considered unworthy of credit and contrary to apostolic tradition.

Despite the historical criticisms, the concept of Aeons resurfaces in modern thought, finding new interpretations and applications in various fields of knowledge and spirituality. In philosophy, the concept of Aeon has been rescued by thinkers who seek alternatives to the mechanistic and reductionist paradigm of modern science, proposing more organic, holistic, and animistic worldviews. Some contemporary philosophers, inspired by the thought of authors such as Carl Jung and Mircea Eliade, explore the concept of Aeon as a primordial archetype of human consciousness, a symbol of psychic totality and the search for meaning and transcendence. In this perspective, the Aeons are not necessarily real spiritual entities, but rather symbolic representations of deep psychic forces and processes, which act in the collective unconscious and shape human experience.

In psychology, especially in Jung's analytical psychology, the concept of Aeon finds resonance in the notion of archetypes and collective symbols. Jung, influenced by Gnosticism and Hermeticism, recognized the importance of symbols and archetypal images in the dynamics of the human psyche and in the journey of individuation. The concept of Aeon, for Jung, can be seen as an archetype of totality, of the integration of opposites, and of the search for psychic unity. The figure of Christ, as a saving Aeon in Gnosis, is interpreted by Jung as a central archetype of the human psyche, a symbol of the Self, the integrating center of the total personality. Jungian psychology, by exploring Gnostic symbols and archetypes, contributes to a deeper understanding of the symbolic and archetypal dimension of the concept of Aeons.

In contemporary spirituality, the concept of Aeons has been rescued and reinterpreted in various currents and movements, from New Age spirituality to neo-

Gnosticism and modern esotericism. In some contexts, the Aeons are seen as real spiritual beings, hierarchies of cosmic intelligences that act as guides and helpers in the spiritual journey. In other contexts, the Aeons are interpreted in a more symbolic and metaphorical way, as representations of divine qualities, archetypal forces, or aspects of cosmic consciousness. The search for connection with the Aeons, through meditation, creative visualization, or ritual practices, becomes a way to expand consciousness, access inner wisdom, and experience the presence of the divine in everyday life.

The relevance and value of the study of Aeons in the 21st century lies in its ability to offer an alternative and enriching perspective on spirituality, cosmology, and the human condition. In a world marked by materialism, rationalism, and fragmentation, the concept of Aeons invites us to rediscover the mystical and symbolic dimension of reality, to recognize the existence of broader and deeper planes of consciousness, and to seek a more direct and meaningful connection with the divine. The study of Aeons can contribute to a revitalization of spirituality in the face of contemporary challenges, offering a path for the search for meaning, for inner transformation, and for reconnection with our own divine essence. Despite historical criticisms and different modern interpretations, the concept of Aeons remains a rich and inspiring legacy of esoteric Christianity, an invitation to explore the depths of consciousness and to seek union with the ultimate mystery of existence.

# Chapter 16
# The Redemptive Mission of Christ

The manifestation of Christ as the Saving Aeon emerges as a decisive milestone in the spiritual trajectory of humanity, introducing a redemptive dynamic that surpasses traditional conceptions of salvation linked to guilt, sin, and the need for atonement. Christ, in this esoteric and Gnostic context, presents himself as a direct emanation of the divine fullness, the Pleroma, carrying in his essence the primordial light and transcendent knowledge capable of breaking the chains of ignorance that keep souls captive in materiality. His coming does not represent merely the descent of a divine envoy to fulfill a historical prophecy, but rather, the irruption of a cosmic presence that introduces into the fallen world the real possibility of reintegration with the divine. This Christ, clothed in the ineffable light of the Pleroma, is not a distant or inaccessible figure, but a cosmic mediator whose mission is to awaken the divine that lies dormant in each soul, reminding it of its celestial origin and leading it back to the eternal source. Thus, his redemptive mission is not limited to historical events or external rituals, but unfolds within each human being, in the awakening of their divine spark and in the progressive recognition of their true spiritual identity.

By assuming his mission in the material world, Christ does not limit himself to teaching doctrines or moral precepts, but embodies in his own manifestation the revelation of Gnosis, the secret and transformative knowledge that leads the soul to liberation. His presence is, in itself, a rupture in the fabric of illusory reality, a luminous tear that allows souls captured by ignorance and forgetfulness to glimpse the essential truth hidden under layers of conditioning and suffering. The action of Christ as the Saving Aeon transcends the written word and oral tradition; he acts as a living bridge between the Pleroma and the fallen world, offering each soul the possibility of directly accessing the primordial light, without intermediaries or rigid religious structures. His redemption does not consist in satisfying an external divine justice or rescuing humanity from eternal condemnation, but in dissolving the illusions that sustain human suffering and the incessant cycle of birth and death, allowing each being to recognize their divine filiation and return, conscious and awakened, to communion with the Ineffable.

The redemptive mission of Christ, therefore, reveals itself as an inner journey of self-knowledge and spiritual awakening, where each soul is called to transcend the illusions of the ego and the sensory world to recognize itself as a direct expression of the divine light. This redemption, based on Gnosis, does not depend on external beliefs or adherence to dogmas and rituals, but on the direct experience of the spiritual truth that Christ embodies and reveals. He is simultaneously teacher, path, and redemptive presence, offering himself as a luminous mirror in which each soul can glimpse its own divine essence. Through this recognition, the soul recovers its primordial memory, remembers its true origin, and begins the process of spiritual ascension, returning to the Pleroma through the path of knowledge and integration with the divine. In this sense, the redemptive mission of Christ the Saving Aeon is not just a localized historical event, but a permanent and timeless invitation to humanity to awaken from its existential sleep, recognize the divine spark within itself, and, through Gnosis, consciously reintegrate into the fullness of the absolute Being.

The divine nature of Christ, as the Saving Aeon, resides in his primordial origin in the Pleroma, the realm of divine fullness. In Gnostic cosmology, Christ is not a creature or a created being, but rather an emanation of the Supreme Divinity itself, sharing in its eternal and immutable nature. This divine origin confers upon Christ a unique authority and power, placing him on a higher level than all creatures of the material world and even other spiritual hierarchies inferior to the Pleroma. Christ, as an Aeon, exists from before the creation of the material world, inhabiting the realm of uncreated light and participating in the divine fullness in his primordial origin. His coming to the material world, therefore, is not an incarnation in the traditional sense, but rather a manifestation, a descent of his divine presence into a temporal and material context, with a specific redemptive purpose.

The role of Christ as the Saving Aeon manifests itself primarily in his redemptive mission. In the Gnostic perspective, the redemption of humanity does not primarily refer to salvation from eternal damnation or the remission of sins through vicarious sacrifice, but rather to liberation from the ignorance and illusion that imprison the human soul in the material world. Humanity, in the Gnostic view, is in a state of spiritual exile, forgotten of its true divine nature and alienated from its origin in the Pleroma. The mission of Christ as the Saving Aeon is to awaken human consciousness to this reality, to reveal Gnosis, the saving knowledge, and to offer the path for the return to the realm of light.

The redemption offered by the Aeon Christ is not, therefore, a salvation "from" something external, such as sin or divine wrath, but rather a salvation "to" something internal, the awakening of consciousness and the realization of divine identity. Christ does not sacrifice himself to appease divine justice or to pay a debt incurred by humanity, but rather manifests himself in the world to transmit Gnosis, the knowledge that liberates the soul from ignorance and leads it back to its primordial origin. Gnostic redemption is, essentially, a process of self-knowledge, of discovering the inner divine spark, and of the ascension of consciousness to the higher spiritual dimensions of reality. Christ, as the Saving Aeon, is the guide and facilitator of this process, the master who reveals the path and the companion who accompanies the soul's journey in search of Gnosis.

The message of Christ, in the Gnostic perspective, centers on the revelation of Gnosis as the path of spiritual liberation. The teachings of Christ, preserved in Gnostic texts, are not limited to moral precepts or religious dogmas, but rather to principles and insights that aim to awaken consciousness and illuminate the mind to spiritual truth. Christ invites to inner searching, self-knowledge, contemplation, and mystical experience as ways of accessing Gnosis and redemption. His message is a call to a radical transformation of consciousness, to a change of perspective that transcends the limited and illusory view of the material world and opens up to the vastness and depth of spiritual reality. Salvation, in the message of Christ the Saving Aeon, is a state of being, a condition of awakened and enlightened consciousness, achieved through Gnosis and union with the divine.

It is important to contrast the redemptive mission of the Aeon Christ with the predominant view of redemption in exoteric or orthodox Christianity. While orthodox Christianity emphasizes faith in Christ as an atoning sacrifice, divine grace as an unmerited gift, and participation in the sacraments as means of salvation, esoteric Christianity, through the figure of Christ the Saving Aeon, proposes a path of redemption intrinsically linked to knowledge, mystical experience, and inner transformation. Gnosis, and not dogmatic faith or mere ritual observance, emerges as the central element of Gnostic soteriology. Redemption is not seen as an external event or a juridical act of divine forgiveness, but rather as an internal process of awakening consciousness and realizing the divine nature of the soul.

The figure of Christ as the Saving Aeon, therefore, represents a unique and enriching perspective on redemption in the Christian context. It offers a path of salvation that values the pursuit of knowledge, mystical experience, and the transformation of consciousness, resonating with the human thirst for transcendence and a deeper meaning in life. The message of Christ the Saving Aeon invites us to go beyond the external forms of religion, to seek the direct experience of spiritual truth, and to tread the path of Gnosis towards liberation and union with the Supreme Divinity. The understanding of Christ as the Saving Aeon opens new avenues for the exploration of the Christian faith, unveiling mystical and esoteric dimensions that enrich its message and expand its transformative potential. The figure of Christ the Saving Aeon remains a luminous guide on the soul's journey in search of Gnosis and spiritual redemption, offering a vision of hope and liberation for humanity imprisoned in the illusion of the material world.

# Chapter 17
# Christ in the Aeonic Hierarchy

Christ occupies a position of profound significance within the structure of the Pleroma, not merely as one Aeon among many, but as a direct expression of the divine will to return lost emanations to their original state of fullness. In his primordial essence, Christ embodies the very bridge between the infinitude of the Supreme Source and the multiplicity of the Aeons, bearing not only the light of divine knowledge but also the capacity to reintegrate the fragmented into the One. His position in the Pleroma is not merely a matter of hierarchy, but reflects the cosmic function he is destined to perform: to restore harmony where imbalance has taken hold, to reveal the path of spiritual ascension, and to act as a living echo of the divine mind. This functional centrality of Christ does not place him in a position of spiritual tyranny or authoritarian supremacy, but as an axial point through which the other spiritual emanations can realign themselves with their origin. He is, simultaneously, the perfect reflection of Unity within plurality and the outstretched hand of fullness to rescue what has fallen into forgetfulness and dispersion.

The singular nature of Christ is also revealed in his restorative function in the face of the drama of the original fragmentation. When Sophia, in her yearning to directly know the Source, precipitated the disturbance that gave rise to matter and the distance between the Pleroma and the lower world, it was through the emanation of Christ that the divine order found its way to restoration. Christ, therefore, is not just another Aeon among emanations of light, but the very manifestation of the compassion and redemptive intelligence of the Pleroma, the one who takes responsibility for guiding all lost souls back to the consciousness of their origin. This restorative and reconciling role does not diminish the other Aeons, but highlights the specific function of Christ as a direct mediator between the Ineffable and the manifest. He is the voice that translates primordial silence into accessible revelation; he is the light that traverses the shadows of ignorance without being contaminated by them; he is the incarnate knowledge that rescues the divine spark buried in dense matter.

Although he shares the same divine essence of all the Aeons, Christ's specific mission as revealer and redeemer highlights him as a privileged expression of the Supreme Will. Unlike Aeons whose function is to preserve harmony in the Pleroma or sustain the invisible structures of creation, Christ is the one who crosses the boundaries of the Pleroma, entering the domains of matter and forgetfulness, without losing his connection to the Source. This crossing, carried out out of love for the lost emanations, constitutes the heart of his mission: to remind the human soul of its true origin, to dissolve the veils of illusion, and to reopen the path of spiritual ascension. Christ is, thus, the synthesis of all paths, the map and the guide, the living presence of fullness within limitation, eternally offering himself as a mirror in which each soul can contemplate its own hidden light and rediscover its path of return to the Pleroma.

One strand of Gnostic thought tends to place Christ in a position of hierarchical superiority within the Pleroma. In this perspective, Christ is considered a primary Aeon, emanated directly from the Monad or one of the first divine syzygies, occupying a place of prominence and preeminence in relation to the other Aeons. This hierarchical superiority of Christ is often justified by his unique and universal redemptive mission, his role as the revealer of Gnosis and guide to the salvation of humanity, and his special proximity to the Supreme Divinity. Christ, in this view, would be the "firstborn" among the Aeons, the most direct and powerful representative of the divine will in the cosmos, the supreme mediator between the Pleroma and the material world.

Gnostic texts such as the Gospel of Truth and the Apocryphon of John, although not explicitly detailing a rigid Aeonic hierarchy, suggest a special position for Christ. In the Gospel of Truth, Christ is described as the voice of the Father, the revealer of the divine mystery, and the bearer of the knowledge that liberates from ignorance. In the Apocryphon of John, Christ is presented as a primordial emanation, manifested to correct Sophia's fault and restore cosmic order, indicating a singular role and superior divine authority.

These texts, and others from the Nag Hammadi library, can be interpreted as corroborating a view of Christ as an Aeon with an elevated hierarchical status within the Pleroma, although without explicitly detailing a rigid and immutable hierarchy.

Another strand of Gnostic thought, on the other hand, tends to emphasize the fundamental equality between Christ and the other Aeons, placing him on a plane of parity in relation to the other spiritual beings of the Pleroma. In this perspective, Christ is seen as one Aeon among others, sharing the same divine nature and the same origin in the emanation of the Monad. His specificity would reside not in a hierarchical superiority, but in his particular redemptive mission and his function as the revealer of Gnosis, which distinguishes him from the other Aeons in terms of role and cosmic action, but not in terms of divine essence or ontological status. In this view, all Aeons, including Christ, are manifestations of the same Supreme Divinity, expressions of the same divine fullness, and participate equally in the eternal and immutable nature of the Pleroma.

Texts such as the Gospel of Philip and the Gospel of Thomas, in their less hierarchical and more Gnosis-experience-focused approaches, can be interpreted as corroborating a view of equality among the Aeons. The Gospel of Philip, with its emphasis on mystical union with Christ and the experience of the Gnostic sacraments, seems to suggest direct access to divinity through Gnosis, without necessarily emphasizing a rigidly defined hierarchy between Christ and the other spiritual beings. The Gospel of Thomas, with its secret sayings of Jesus, focuses on the inner search and the realization of the divine identity within each individual, suggesting a path of enlightenment that transcends external hierarchies and focuses on the direct experience of spiritual truth. These texts can be interpreted as indicating a view of Christ as a guide and an example on the path of Gnosis, but not necessarily as a figure hierarchically superior to the other Aeons in terms of divine essence.

The question of Christ's superiority or equality in the Aeonic Hierarchy can be seen as a matter of emphasis and theological perspective within the diversity of Gnostic thought. Both views, superiority and equality, can be found in different Gnostic texts and traditions, reflecting different ways of understanding the figure of Christ and the structure of the Pleroma. The view of Christ's hierarchical superiority may emphasize his uniqueness and importance for Gnostic soteriology, highlighting his unique role as the revealer of Gnosis and guide to redemption. The view of equality between Christ and the other Aeons, on the other hand, may emphasize the unity of the Supreme Divinity and the fundamental equality of all spiritual beings emanating from it, highlighting the accessibility of Gnosis and the possibility of union with the divine for all spiritual seekers.

It is important to note that, even in the strands that emphasize Christ's hierarchical superiority, this superiority does not imply authoritarian domination or a hierarchy of power in the worldly sense. The Aeonic hierarchy, in its essence, is a hierarchy of function and of irradiation of divine light, not a hierarchy of power or oppression. Christ, even in a prominent position, acts in harmony and cooperation with the other Aeons, in pursuit of the common good and the realization of the divine plan. The Aeonic hierarchy reflects the order and organization inherent in the spiritual cosmos, but also its unity and interconnection.

The discussion about Christ's place in the Aeonic Hierarchy is not merely an abstract theological debate, but a reflection that has implications for spiritual practice and for the understanding of the Gnostic journey. If Christ is seen as hierarchically superior, devotion to and invocation of Christ as guide and savior can be emphasized as a privileged path to Gnosis and redemption. If Christ is seen as equal to the other Aeons in divine essence, the search for Gnosis can be understood as a broader and more inclusive path, involving connection with different Aeons and exploration of various dimensions of spiritual reality.

The question of Christ's superiority or equality in the Aeonic Hierarchy remains open, reflecting the diversity and richness of Gnostic thought. Both perspectives offer valuable insights into the figure of Christ and the Gnostic spiritual cosmos, inviting deep reflection and a personal search for understanding of the divine truth. The exploration of Christ's place in the Aeonic Hierarchy allows us to appreciate the complexity and nuance of esoteric Christianity and its unique view of the figure of Christ as a Savior Aeon, a luminous guide in the soul's journey in search of Gnosis and union with the divine.

# Chapter 18
# The Mission of Christ in the Material World

The descent of the Aeon Christ into the material world represents the highest expression of divine compassion for humanity, imprisoned within the gears of a cosmos marked by forgetfulness and fragmentation. His coming to the plane of matter does not result from an external imposition or an arbitrary cosmic obligation, but rather from a conscious decision rooted in the very essence of the Pleroma, where the fullness of divine light, recognizing the pain of the exiled sparks, voluntarily emanates the Savior to rescue what was lost. Christ does not invade the material world as a conqueror or judge, but enters the fabric of corrupted creation with gentleness and the strength of one who carries the truth that dissolves error, the light that dispels darkness, and the primordial memory that rescues the meaning hidden behind illusion. His mission, therefore, is a silent summons, a loving call to sleeping souls, to recognize their forgotten origin and awaken to the living knowledge that, once accepted, breaks the chains of existential imprisonment.

Upon penetrating the spheres of matter, Christ does not assume an arbitrary or contingent form, but adopts a manifestation compatible with the psychic and spiritual reality of fallen humanity. His presence among humans is not limited to a physical incarnation, but expresses the unique ability to project his essence into a vehicle suitable for the sensible world, while preserving his direct and uninterrupted connection with the Pleroma. This dual rootedness – simultaneously present in the world and linked to the Ineffable – gives Christ the ability to act as a living bridge between the higher and lower realms of existence, offering humanity not only words or doctrines, but the very embodied experience of the saving presence. Every gesture, every teaching, and every act of his earthly mission reverberates with this connection, not as an abstract discourse, but as the very vibration of the Pleroma that infiltrates the heart of fallen creation, awakening in it the echo of the forgotten origin.

The essence of Christ's mission in the material world is the restoration of spiritual memory, dormant in human souls, buried under layers of sensory, ideological, and psychic conditioning cultivated by the Archons and reinforced by the very flow of material existence. He does not offer ready-made formulas or external paths of salvation, but ignites in each soul that crosses his path the remembrance that the light already dwells within, that the divine is not a distant point in the firmament, but an immanent reality waiting to be recognized. His redemptive mission consists in reactivating this primordial memory through Gnosis, a living and direct knowledge, not mediated by dogmas or external authorities, but accessible directly in the innermost core of the soul itself. From this recollection, each awakened human being begins to walk a journey of reintegration, where consciousness itself becomes the temple of revelation and material life, once a prison and labyrinth, is transformed into a sacred space for the manifestation of the recovered divine. Thus, Christ's mission is not limited to an era, a people, or a specific tradition; it resonates as a universal and timeless call, echoing eternally within each soul that dares to remember its true nature and turn to the primordial light from which it came.

The mission of Christ in the material world has as its primary objective the revelation of Gnosis. In the Gnostic view, ignorance is the root of all human suffering, the fundamental cause of spiritual alienation and imprisonment in matter. Humanity, obscured by the illusion of the material world and the machinations of the Archons, has forgotten its divine origin, its spiritual identity, and the path of return to the Pleroma. Christ, as an emissary of the realm of light, descends into the world to dispel this ignorance, to break the veil of illusion, and to reveal Gnosis, the liberating knowledge that illuminates the mind and ignites the flame of spiritual consciousness. Gnosis is not merely intellectual information or theoretical doctrine, but rather a transformative experience, an intuitive and experiential knowledge of divine truth that works a metamorphosis in the human soul, awakening it to transcendent reality.

The revelation of Gnosis by Christ in the material world takes on various forms and expressions, reflecting the richness and complexity of the Gnostic message. Christ manifests himself through teachings, transmitting parables, maxims, and discourses that challenge linear and rational understanding, inviting introspection and the search for a deeper meaning. The Apocryphal Gospels and the Nag Hammadi texts preserve these esoteric teachings of Christ, revealing a message that transcends conventional morality and religious dogmas, focusing on inner transformation and self-knowledge as paths to spiritual liberation. The teachings of Christ, from the Gnostic perspective, are tools for awakening consciousness, for breaking with the conditioning of the material mind, and for opening oneself to the intuition of divine truth.

In addition to teachings, Christ also reveals Gnosis through signs and examples, demonstrating in his own life and in his actions the path of spiritual transformation and union with the divine. The miracles of Christ, interpreted symbolically in Gnosis, are not mere supernatural prodigies, but rather manifestations of the divine power that resides in Christ and that is potentially present in every human being. Healing, resurrection, and other miraculous acts of Christ symbolically represent the healing of the soul from ignorance, the resurrection of the spirit to eternal life, and the manifestation of the divine power that resides in each spiritual spark. Christ's own example of life, his compassion, his love, and his surrender to the divine will, serve as a model and an incentive for humanity's spiritual journey.

Christ's mission in the material world is also directed towards the spiritual awakening of humanity. The Gnosis revealed by Christ is not passive or merely intellectual knowledge, but rather a call to action, an invitation to the transformation of consciousness and the active search for spiritual liberation. Christ not only transmits Gnosis, but also awakens sleeping souls, stimulating the longing for divine truth and the search for return to the Pleroma. This spiritual awakening is an inner process, a metamorphosis of consciousness that begins with the recognition of one's own ignorance and the longing for truth, and that develops through the practice of meditation, contemplation, introspection, and the living of Gnostic teachings. Spiritual awakening is, in essence, a rebirth of the soul to true life, an exit from the sleep of illusion, and an entry into the light of Gnosis.

Christ's call to spiritual awakening resonates through the centuries, inviting each individual to take responsibility for their own spiritual journey and to seek Gnosis as a path of liberation. Christ's message is not for an intellectual elite or a select group of initiates, but rather for all humanity, for all those who yearn for truth and spiritual liberation. Christ offers Gnosis to all who are willing to receive it, to all who open their hearts and minds to his transformative message. Spiritual awakening, in the Gnostic perspective, is an inalienable right of every human being, a possibility inherent in their divine nature, and a response to the call of the Savior Aeon Christ.

Christ's mission in the material world, revealing Gnosis and promoting spiritual awakening, is not limited to the historical context of the first century or to the figure of Jesus of Nazareth. In the Gnostic perspective, the presence and influence of the Aeon Christ transcend time and space, manifesting continuously throughout history and in the inner experience of each spiritual seeker. Christ, as Savior Aeon, remains present in the world, inspiring, guiding, and supporting those who dedicate themselves to the search for Gnosis and the journey of return to the Pleroma. His redemptive mission continues to unfold through the centuries, through the teachings preserved in Gnostic texts, through the spiritual inspiration that resonates in awakened hearts, and through the practice of Gnosis as a living path of transformation and liberation.

The exploration of the Mission of Christ in the Material World reveals the essence of Gnostic soteriology and the depth of the message of esoteric Christianity. Christ, as Savior Aeon, emerges as the revealer of Gnosis, the guide to spiritual awakening, and the bearer of the promise of redemption for exiled humanity. His mission is not limited to a past historical event, but rather to a living and transformative presence that continues to act in the world and in human consciousness, inviting all to walk the path of Gnosis and awaken to their true divine identity and their eternal destiny in the Pleroma. The message of Christ in the material world resonates as a call to liberation from ignorance, to the search for truth, and to the realization of the spiritual potential inherent in every human being, illuminating the journey of the soul towards Gnosis and union with the divine.

# Chapter 19
# The Gospel of Truth and the Aeon Christ

The Gospel of Truth reveals itself as a work of profound spiritual beauty and a vibrant testimony to the mission of the Aeon Christ as the bearer of light and Gnosis, translating into poetic words the eternal call of the Supreme Divinity to humanity exiled in the material world. In this gospel, the figure of Christ transcends historical linearity and the limits of a particular incarnation, presenting himself as the very voice of the Father, the emanation of the primordial truth that resonates in the depths of every soul seeking the way back to the divine home. Christ's function, as the revealer of the fullness of the Pleroma, is not only to transmit a set of doctrines or moral prescriptions, but to lead human consciousness back to the living memory of its spiritual origin, tearing away the veil of ignorance that separates the being from its divine source. His mission, therefore, is not limited to correcting behaviors or restoring a broken covenant, but to illuminate the heart obscured by forgetfulness, so that each soul, upon recognizing the truth of its essence, may rediscover for itself the path of return.

The work describes the material world as a territory where ignorance reigns supreme, keeping souls imprisoned in distorted perceptions about themselves and about ultimate reality. In this landscape of forgetfulness and suffering, the Aeon Christ descends as an expression of the Father's unconditional love, not to condemn or punish, but to remind and heal. He appears as the visible manifestation of the primordial love that yearns for reconciliation between the totality and its dispersed parts, offering himself as the way and the mirror in which each soul can see, reflected, its true spiritual face. Ignorance, the root of all suffering, is not here a moral fault or an inherited guilt, but an existential condition resulting from alienation from the divine. Christ, with his presence and his word, dispels the darkness of this ignorance by offering Gnosis—a knowledge that is not simply an accumulation of concepts, but the direct awakening of the divine spark that dwells in every being.

The truth revealed by Christ, according to the Gospel of Truth, is inseparable from love. Love and knowledge walk hand in hand as complementary forces in the process of redemption. The Father's love, which overflows from the Pleroma to the densest layers of creation, manifests itself in the sending of Christ as an act of deep compassion, where the divine bends down to embrace its forgotten emanations. This love does not judge or demand reparation, but invites and welcomes, offering the recognition of each soul's true nature as an indivisible part of the divine fullness. At the same time, this love is realized in the revealing knowledge that Christ transmits: the knowledge that separation is an illusion, that exile is only a dream, and that the truth of being has always been intact, hidden under layers of fear, confusion, and deception. Thus, the mission of the Aeon Christ, as echoed in this gospel, is to return to humanity its lost spiritual vision, so that the Father's love and the light of Gnosis may restore harmony between the Creator and his dispersed emanations, dissolving the abyss of separation and reintegrating each soul into the eternal unity of the Pleroma.

The Gospel of Truth begins with a fundamental statement that sets the tone and purpose of the text: "The Gospel of Truth is joy for those who have received the grace to know [the Father of truth], in the name of the Son, who is Jesus Christ." This opening sentence already reveals the central themes of the gospel: truth, knowledge, grace, love, joy, and the central figure of Jesus Christ as the vehicle of revelation. The gospel presents itself as a message of joy and liberation, intended for those who are receptive to divine truth and who seek saving knowledge.

A recurring theme in the Gospel of Truth is the Father's love as the driving force of redemption. The Father is described as the primordial source of all being, an overflowing love that yearns for reconciliation with his creation exiled in ignorance. The Father is not a severe judge or a punishing power, but rather a loving parent who seeks the return of his lost children to the home of light. This paternal love is manifested in the coming of the Aeon Christ, sent into the world to reveal the truth and offer the way back to the Father. The Father's love is the basis of Christ's message, the foundation of the Gnostic hope of redemption, and the engine of the spiritual journey in search of Gnosis.

Knowledge (Gnosis), in the Gospel of Truth, is not just intellectual knowledge, but rather a transformative experience that frees the soul from ignorance and reconnects it with its divine origin. Ignorance is described as the fundamental cause of human suffering, the root of spiritual alienation and imprisonment in the material world. The knowledge of the truth, revealed by Christ, dispels this ignorance, breaking the bonds of illusion and opening the eyes of the soul to spiritual reality. Gnosis is a knowledge that heals, that liberates, that transforms consciousness, and that leads to union with the Father. It is a knowledge that is experienced in the heart and soul, and not just in the rational mind.

The Aeon Christ, in the Gospel of Truth, is presented as the revealer of the Father and the bearer of Gnosis. He is the beloved Son of the Father, sent into the world to manifest his love and to offer the way of redemption. Christ is not described in terms of historical events or biographical details, but rather in his spiritual essence and in his redemptive function. He is the word of the Father, the manifestation of truth, the light that dispels the darkness of ignorance, and the guide who leads back home. The figure of Christ in the Gospel of Truth is essentially symbolic and archetypal, representing the divine principle of revelation and redemption, manifested in the world to awaken humanity to its true spiritual identity.

The voice of Christ in the Gospel of Truth is the voice of a compassionate and loving guide, who invites to inner searching and the awakening of consciousness. Christ does not impose dogmas or external precepts, but rather offers a path of self-knowledge and inner transformation, through Gnosis and love. His language is poetic, metaphorical, and symbolic, directed to the heart and intuition, and not just to the rational mind. Christ speaks in parables and allegories, inviting deep reflection and the search for a deeper meaning in his words. His voice is a voice of hope, of comfort, of encouragement, and of calling to spiritual awakening.

In the Gospel of Truth, reconciliation with the Father emerges as the ultimate goal of the spiritual journey and the redemptive mission of Christ. Humanity, exiled and alienated from the Father, yearns to return to its divine origin and to rediscover the primordial unity. Christ, through the revelation of Gnosis and the manifestation of the Father's love, offers the path to this reconciliation, opening the doors of the Pleroma and inviting all to return to the home of light. Reconciliation is not just a divine forgiveness or a restoration of a previous state, but rather a profound transformation of consciousness, a reintegration into the divine fullness, and a realization of the primordial unity between the Father and his creation.

The Gospel of Truth, in its central message of love and knowledge, resonates deeply with the human search for meaning, transcendence, and spiritual reconciliation. Its presentation of the Aeon Christ as the revealer of the Father and the guide to Gnosis offers a path of hope and liberation for exiled humanity, inviting all to awaken to the divine truth and to walk the journey back to the home of light. The voice of Christ in the Gospel of Truth remains as a luminous beacon in the night of ignorance, guiding spiritual seekers towards Gnosis and union with the Supreme Divinity, through love and knowledge. The analysis of the Gospel of Truth reveals the beauty and depth of the Gnostic message, and its ability to inspire and transform the lives of those who open themselves to its ancient wisdom.

# Chapter 20
# The Secret Teachings of the Christ Aeon

The secret teachings of the Christ Aeon, preserved in works such as the Gospel of Thomas, reveal a profound layer of the redemptive mission that transcends historical narratives and penetrates directly into the core of individual spiritual experience. These teachings were not intended for the masses, but for those whose souls had already awakened to spiritual restlessness, to the subtle call that echoes from the divine spark imprisoned in the world of form. Christ, as the revealing Aeon, did not offer mere words of comfort or moral rules for human coexistence; he transmitted hidden keys, fragments of a primordial knowledge capable of undoing the web of illusions woven by the Archons, leading each seeker to the direct recognition of their divine identity and their origin in the Pleroma. These secret teachings, therefore, do not function as simple maxims of wisdom, but as spiritual portals that, when correctly understood, unfold within consciousness, awakening the silent and luminous knowledge that has always been present, though forgotten.

The essence of these teachings lies in the radical reorientation of the perception of reality. Christ does not point to a distant God, located outside or above the world, but to a sacred presence that permeates the very being of the seeker. The idea that the Kingdom is within and without—but invisible to eyes conditioned by deception—subverts the traditional religious paradigm and returns to the individual the responsibility for their own redemption. This vision coincides with the structure of the Gnostic cosmos, where the Pleroma is not just a remote dwelling reserved for the pure, but a dimension accessible to awakened consciousness, a vibrant reality awaiting the gaze purified by Gnosis. Christ, therefore, does not place himself as an intermediary between the human and the divine, but as the one who teaches the path of self-revelation, in which each soul rediscovers its divine filiation and its right to reintegration into fullness.

In the secret sayings, this pedagogy of awakening is revealed through parables that dissolve certainties, aphorisms that break with dualistic logic, and invitations to radical introspection, where inner silence becomes the dwelling place of truth. Christ does not offer linear explanations or ready-made truths; he plants questions that ferment in the soul until the inner spark—hidden under layers of fear, beliefs, and conditioning—rekindles itself. Each seemingly simple saying is a key to spiritual activation, the full meaning of which is only revealed as the seeker walks towards their own essence. This esoteric pedagogy, at once compassionate and challenging, is the direct expression of Christ's Aeonic mission: to lead each soul to the memory of its true identity, without impositions, but through the loving invitation to discover the sacred that dwells within it.

Thus, the secret teachings of the Christ Aeon remain as living echoes of the primordial voice that, even under the veil of forgetfulness, continues to call each soul to its origin and its fullness in the Pleroma.

The Gospel of Thomas begins with a statement that defines its nature and purpose: "These are the secret words that Jesus, the Living One, spoke and Didymus Judas Thomas recorded." This opening sentence emphasizes the secret character of the teachings, the authority of Jesus as "the Living One," and the role of Thomas as the transmitter of the esoteric tradition. The term "secret words" suggests that the teachings contained in the gospel are not for public or exoteric consumption, but rather intended for a more restricted circle of initiated disciples, capable of understanding the depth and hidden meaning of Christ's words.

The "secret" nature of the teachings of the Gospel of Thomas resonates with the very essence of Gnosis, the esoteric and transformative knowledge that is central to Gnostic Christianity. Gnosis is not superficial knowledge or accessible to the common rational mind, but rather a deep and intuitive knowing that requires discernment, introspection, and a mind open to spiritual reality. The secret sayings of Jesus in the Gospel of Thomas challenge literal and exoteric interpretation, inviting the spiritual seeker to go beyond the surface of the words, to delve into the depths of their hidden meaning, and to awaken to the spiritual truth that lies behind the symbolic and enigmatic language.

The interpretation of the sayings of Jesus in the Gospel of Thomas in light of the Aeonic perspective reveals profound connections between the secret teachings and Gnostic cosmology. Many sayings, when understood through the Aeonic lens, point to the divine nature of the human being, the reality of the Pleroma, and the path of Gnosis as a return to the divine origin. For example, saying 3, which states: "If those who lead you say to you, 'See, the Kingdom is in the sky!', then the birds of the sky will precede you. If they say to you, 'It is in the sea!', then the fish will precede you. Rather, the Kingdom is within you and it is outside of you," resonates with the Gnostic view of the Kingdom of God not as a geographical place or an eschatological future, but rather as a present and immanent spiritual reality, accessible through inner searching and the awakening of consciousness. The Kingdom, in the Aeonic perspective, can be understood as the Pleroma, the divine fullness that transcends the material world, but which also manifests in resonance with the inner divine spark present in each human being.

Another significant example is saying 50: "Jesus said, 'If they say to you, 'Where did you come from?', say to them, 'We came from the light, the place where the light came into being on its own.' If they say to you, 'Who are you?', say to them, 'We are its children, and we are the elect of the Living Father.' If they ask you, 'What is the sign of your Father in you?', say to them, 'It is movement and repose.'" This saying concisely expresses the divine origin of humanity, its provenance from the realm of light, and its filiation to the Living Father, central concepts in Aeonic cosmology. The answer about the "sign of the Father" as "movement and repose" can be interpreted esoterically as the dynamic of emanation and return to the Pleroma, the constant flow of divine energy that manifests in the cosmos and the yearning of the human soul for rest in divine unity.

The search for the Inner Kingdom and the realization of divine identity are recurring themes in the Gospel of Thomas, and they harmonize deeply with the Aeonic perspective. Many sayings emphasize the importance of introspection, self-knowledge, and the search for truth within oneself as the path to Gnosis and union with the divine. The Kingdom of God is not something external to be achieved in the future, but rather an inner reality to be discovered and experienced in the present. Divine identity is not something to be acquired or deserved, but rather an essential nature to be recognized and manifested in fullness. The Gospel of Thomas, under the Aeonic lens, invites an inner journey of awakening and self-discovery, where Gnosis is the map and the Christ Aeon is the guide.

The Gospel of Thomas, with its secret and enigmatic teachings, offers a valuable and complementary perspective for understanding the Christ Aeon and the Gnostic message. Its concise and provocative sayings challenge the rational mind and stimulate intuition, inviting the spiritual seeker to go beyond literality and penetrate the depths of the divine mystery. The search for the Inner Kingdom and the realization of divine identity, central themes of the Gospel of Thomas, resonate with the Gnostic journey of return to the Pleroma and with the search for union with the Supreme Divinity. The Gospel of Thomas, interpreted in light of the Aeonic perspective, reveals itself as a precious guide on the path of Gnosis, a concise and profound map for the realization of spiritual truth and liberation from the illusion of the material world. The exploration of the secret sayings of the Gospel of Thomas enriches our understanding of esoteric Christianity and the transformative message of the Christ Aeon, inviting us to delve into the depths of self-knowledge and awaken to our own divine nature.

# Chapter 21
# Aeonic Christ and Historical Jesus

A profound understanding of the figure of Christ, within the esoteric Christian tradition, requires an approach that transcends the conventional and literal reading of scriptures and historical accounts. Christ, in the esoteric perspective, is not merely a specific character inserted in the socio-political context of 1st century Palestine, but rather the manifestation of an eternal spiritual reality that permeates the cosmos and the human soul since before the foundation of the material world. This conception allows us to understand Christ as a supreme expression of the divine creative energy, the manifestation of the primordial Logos that acts as a link between the Pleroma—the realm of divine fullness—and the phenomenal world, marked by fragmentation and spiritual ignorance. In this sense, the figure of Christ transcends the limits of a biography or a historical chronology to reveal itself as an atemporal principle of redemption, of reintegration of the human soul to its divine source, and of revelation of the true spiritual nature of existence. The cosmic dimension of Christ does not annul or replace his historical presence in Jesus of Nazareth, but expands this presence, offering it a meaning that encompasses both the human condition and the divine vocation of humanity.

By examining the distinction and complementarity between the Aeonic Christ and the Historical Jesus, esoteric Christianity proposes an integrative vision that harmonizes the concrete experience of Jesus, as an incarnate master, with the archetypal reality of Christ as a universal divine principle. Jesus of Nazareth, with his life trajectory, his words, and his actions, embodied and expressed in his own existence the attributes and the mission of the Aeonic Christ, becoming a conscious vehicle of this divine force that transcends space and time. Thus, each stage of Jesus' life—from his birth in humble circumstances to his passion and resurrection—acquires a symbolic and archetypal dimension, reflecting, in historical language, the deep movements of the soul in its return to its divine essence. This intertwining between history and myth, between biographical event and cosmic mystery, should not be read as a contradiction, but as a key to reading that allows us to penetrate the hidden layers of Christianity and access its deepest esoteric message. The figure of Jesus, therefore, is not just a prophet or religious reformer, but the very embodiment of the Logos, who chose the human condition to reveal, through his presence and teaching, the path of the reintegration of the human being to the divine.

This integrative perspective allows the spiritual seeker to understand that the spiritual journey proposed by esoteric Christianity is not an escape from reality or a denial of history, but a resignification of human existence itself in the light of Gnosis. Each human being, upon contemplating the figure of Christ, is invited to recognize in themselves this same divine spark, this same latent Christic potential that awaits to be awakened. The apparent duality between Aeonic Christ and Historical Jesus dissolves as the seeker realizes that the true goal of the spiritual path is the direct experience of the inner Christ—the realization of this divine presence in their own consciousness and daily life. The Aeonic Christ, as an eternal archetype, and the Historical Jesus, as a temporal and incarnate manifestation of this archetype, become two poles of the same spiritual reality: the universal call to Gnosis, to the reintegration of the soul to its divine principle, and to the overcoming of the illusions of the ego and matter. Therefore, understanding the relationship between Aeonic Christ and Historical Jesus is not just a theological or intellectual matter, but a practical and experiential key for those who tread the inner path of seeking the Supreme Truth.

The Aeonic Christ, as explored in previous chapters, represents the figure of Christ within the Gnostic cosmology. He is understood as a Savior Aeon, a direct emanation of the Supreme Divinity, an inhabitant of the Pleroma, and a bearer of Gnosis. The Aeonic Christ transcends the temporal and historical dimension, existing since before the creation of the material world and participating in divine eternity. His coming into the material world, in the Gnostic perspective, is not primarily a biographical event, but rather a cosmic manifestation, an act of divine condescension to reveal Gnosis and awaken humanity to its true spiritual nature. The focus on the Aeonic Christ lies, therefore, in his divine nature, redemptive function, and message of saving knowledge.

On the other hand, the Historical Jesus refers to the figure of Jesus of Nazareth as a real and concrete person who lived in the 1st century AD in Palestine. The historical perspective seeks to reconstruct, through textual sources and archaeological evidence, the life, teachings, and sociocultural context of Jesus, considering him as a Jew of his time, immersed in the traditions and expectations of 1st century Judaism. The focus on the Historical Jesus lies, therefore, in his humanity, historical context, and moral and ethical teachings, as they can be reconstructed through critical analysis of historical sources.

It is fundamental to understand that, from the perspective of esoteric Christianity, the distinction between Aeonic Christ and Historical Jesus does not imply opposition or mutual exclusion. The two perspectives are not necessarily incompatible, but rather complementary, offering different angles of vision on the same spiritual reality. Esoteric Christianity does not deny the historicity of Jesus, nor does it disregard the importance of his historical teachings, but seeks to transcend the limitation of a purely historical reading, recognizing the transcendent and archetypal dimension of the figure of Christ, expressed in the concept of the Savior Aeon.

The Aeonic perspective complements the historical view of Jesus by offering a broader cosmological and metaphysical context for his mission and message. By situating Jesus within the Aeonic hierarchy and Gnostic cosmology, esoteric Christianity enriches the understanding of his figure, revealing his divine dimension and his role as a messenger of the Pleroma. The Aeonic perspective allows us to understand Jesus' message not just as a set of moral precepts or a social and religious movement within 1st century Judaism, but as a revelation of Gnosis, a path of spiritual transformation that resonates with the depths of the human soul and with the transcendent reality of the divine realm.

In some points, the Aeonic perspective may distance itself from the historical view of Jesus, especially with regard to certain aspects of the canonical Gospel narrative that are reinterpreted symbolically in Gnosis. For example, the crucifixion and resurrection of Jesus, central events in orthodox Christian theology, may be seen less literally and more symbolically in the Gnostic perspective, as representations of stages of a process of spiritual initiation and transcendence of the limited human condition, rather than historical events to be understood in their factual literalness. This symbolic reinterpretation does not deny the importance of these events in the Christian tradition, but seeks to unveil their esoteric meaning and their value as archetypes of the spiritual journey.

Despite the possible distances and reinterpretations, both perspectives, Aeonic Christ and

Historical Jesus, converge towards a unified spiritual quest, which is the core of esoteric Christianity. Both the contemplation of the transcendent figure of the Aeonic Christ and the reflection on the teachings and life example of the Historical Jesus can lead the spiritual seeker to self-knowledge, transformation of consciousness, and the pursuit of union with the divine. The historical perspective can offer a concrete and accessible starting point for the spiritual journey, anchoring the search for Gnosis in human reality and the historical context of Jesus. The Aeonic perspective, in turn, can elevate the mind and heart to the transcendental dimensions of reality, inspiring the search for a deeper knowledge and a more direct experience of the divine.

The importance of both perspectives lies in their ability to enrich and complement the spiritual quest within esoteric Christianity. To neglect the historical dimension of Jesus would be to ignore the concreteness of his message and the importance of his human example. On the other hand, to limit oneself to a purely historical view of Jesus would be to obscure his divine dimension and the cosmic scope of his redemptive mission. Esoteric Christianity, in its quest for a deeper and more comprehensive understanding of the Christian faith, seeks to integrate both perspectives, recognizing the importance of both the Historical Jesus and the Aeonic Christ for the spiritual journey and for the realization of Gnosis.

The spiritual quest, in the context of esoteric Christianity, is not about adhering to dogmas or repeating formulas of faith, but about treading a path of self-knowledge, inner transformation, and direct experience of the divine. Both the reflection on the Aeonic Christ and the contemplation of the Historical Jesus can be valuable tools in this journey, guiding the spiritual seeker towards Gnosis and union with the Supreme Divinity. The integration of the perspectives of the Aeonic Christ and the Historical Jesus allows for a richer and deeper understanding of the Christian message, paving the way for a more fulfilling, conscious, and transformative spirituality. The figure of Christ, in his multiple dimensions, remains a luminous guide in the human spiritual quest, a beacon of hope, and an invitation to realize the divine potential inherent in every human being.

# Chapter 22
# Path to Salvific Knowledge

The path to salvific knowledge in esoteric Christianity does not present itself as a simple acceptance of doctrines or beliefs passed down from generation to generation, but rather as a profound call to inner searching, to the rediscovery of the true spiritual essence that dwells at the core of every human being. This journey towards Gnosis is, above all, a summons to remember a forgotten divine origin, a return to the primordial state of communion with the Pleroma, from which the soul originally emanates. From the esoteric perspective, human existence in the material world is a condition of forgetfulness, a state of exile in which the soul, enveloped by the veils of illusion and ignorance, loses awareness of its true nature. Salvific knowledge, therefore, is not something external to be acquired or imposed by a religious authority, but the reactivation of a dormant spiritual memory, an inner illumination that rescues the lost connection with the divine. This inner revelation, awakened and guided by the light of the Aeonic Christ, not only frees the soul from its shackles, but reconstructs, within the being itself, the bridge that leads back to divine fullness.

This journey of return is deeply marked by the recognition of the central role of the Aeonic Christ as the bearer and revealer of Gnosis. In esoteric Christianity, Christ is not only the one who teaches or transmits spiritual truths, but the very channel through which Gnosis flows into material existence. He is the living presence of divine light in the fragmented world, the direct emissary of the Pleroma, whose mission is to rescue the divine sparks imprisoned in flesh and mind obscured by illusion. Each teaching, each parable, and each symbolic gesture of Christ contains, in its essence, layers of hidden meanings that far surpass superficial morality and reveal the hidden map of the soul in its journey of ascension. To follow this path means not only to intellectually understand Christ's message, but to embody it in one's own existence, allowing the inner light to progressively unveil the shadows accumulated by the ego and false identifications with the material world. Salvation, therefore, is inseparable from self-knowledge, because to know oneself deeply is to rediscover, amidst the layers of conditioning, the divine spark that vibrates in tune with the Aeonic Christ himself.

The process of approaching salvific knowledge, however, requires a specific inner disposition, marked by an authentic thirst for truth and an unwavering courage to confront one's own deceptions and illusions. Gnosis, in this sense, is not a mere accumulation of hidden or esoteric information, but the direct experience of spiritual truth that transforms not only the way of thinking, but the very being of the one who opens up to it. It is a flame that consumes the impurities accumulated by the conditioned mind and reveals the nakedness of the soul before the divine, gradually leading it to the recognition of its real identity, not as a creature separated or abandoned in the cosmos, but as a direct emanation of the Divine Source. This inner transformation, promoted by Gnosis, dissolves the false separation between creature and Creator, between the lower world and the Pleroma, and reveals that the path, the truth, and the life are inseparably united in the living presence of the Aeonic Christ. The seeker who treads this path, guided by the light of Christ, not only returns to his origin, but becomes, himself, a living channel of that same light, radiating to the fragmented world the echoes of divine truth rediscovered in his own heart.

The intrinsic relationship between the Aeon Christ and Gnosis lies in the fact that Christ is, in his own divine nature, the manifestation of Gnosis in the material world. He not only possesses Gnosis, but *is* Gnosis incarnate, the divine truth manifest in Aeonic form and accessible to human perception. Christ, as an emanation of the Supreme Divinity, shares in the luminous and cognitive nature of the Pleroma, and his coming to the material world has the primary purpose of communicating this Gnosis to humanity asleep in ignorance. Gnosis is not something separate from Christ, but rather the very essence of his message and his redemptive mission.

The Aeon Christ is, therefore, the bearer of Gnosis, the divine messenger who brings salvific knowledge from the Pleroma to the material world. His message is not limited to moral precepts or religious dogmas, but rather to an invitation to awaken consciousness, to seek within, and to experience spiritual truth directly. Christ reveals Gnosis through his teachings, his parables, his symbols, and, above all, through his own example of life, which demonstrates the path of inner transformation and union with the divine. The Gnosis revealed by Christ is not an abstract or theoretical knowledge, but a practical and existential knowledge that transforms the life of the one who welcomes it and lives it.

Gnosis, in turn, is the path to reach the Aeon Christ and to participate in his redemption. It is not a matter of blind faith or dogmatic adherence, but of an active and conscious search for knowledge of the truth, a path of self-knowledge, introspection, and mystical experience. Gnosis is not something that is received passively, but something that is conquered through spiritual effort, inner discipline, and the opening of the mind and heart to divine reality. The Aeon Christ does not demand blind faith, but invites to the search for Gnosis, to spiritual discernment, and to the personal experience of truth.

Gnosis as salvific knowledge is central to Gnostic soteriology. In the Gnostic view, ignorance is the root of all human suffering and the fundamental cause of spiritual alienation. Gnosis, by dispelling this ignorance, frees the soul from the captivity of matter, the illusion of the material world, and the power of the Demiurge. The knowledge of truth, revealed by Christ, is not just intellectual information, but a transformative power that operates a metamorphosis in consciousness, awakening the inner divine spark and reconnecting the soul with its origin in the Pleroma. Salvation, in the Gnostic perspective, is not achieved through external works or religious rites, but through Gnosis, the salvific knowledge that frees the soul from ignorance and leads it back to its divine fullness.

The Aeon Christ, therefore, not only offers Gnosis, but *is* the very path to achieve it. To follow Christ on the path of Gnosis does not mean only to believe in his teachings, but to live them, to practice them, to embody them in one's own life. The path of Gnosis proposed by Christ involves inner searching, meditation, contemplation, purification of the mind and heart, and openness to mystical experience. Christ is not only a master who teaches Gnosis, but also a guide and a companion on the spiritual journey, who accompanies, supports, and illuminates those who dedicate themselves to the search for salvific knowledge.

Gnosis, in the context of the Aeon Christ, is not an arid or merely intellectual knowledge, but a living, loving, and transformative knowledge. It is a knowledge that ignites the fire of spiritual passion, that nourishes the soul with the sap of divine truth, and that leads to the experience of mystical union with the divine. Love and knowledge, on the path of Gnosis proposed by Christ, are not opposites, but complementary and intrinsically interconnected. Love is the driving force of the spiritual search, the soul's yearning for union with the divine, while knowledge is the light that illuminates the path, the discernment that guides the journey, and the wisdom that transforms consciousness. The Aeon Christ, in his message of love and knowledge, offers an integral path of redemption, which encompasses both the intellectual and the affective dimensions of human experience.

The exploration of the intrinsic relationship between the Aeon Christ and Gnosis reveals the essence of Gnostic soteriology and the centrality of salvific knowledge in esoteric Christianity. Christ emerges as the bearer of Gnosis, the master and guide on the path of self-knowledge and spiritual transformation, and the very path to union with the Supreme Divinity. Gnosis, in turn, reveals itself as the key to liberation from ignorance, to the redemption of the soul, and to the return to the Pleroma. The message of the Aeon Christ, centered on Gnosis, invites to an inner journey of searching for truth, of awakening of consciousness, and of realization of the divine potential inherent in every human being. Understanding the relationship between the Aeon Christ and Gnosis is fundamental to treading the path of Gnostic spirituality and to experiencing the transformation and liberation that salvific knowledge offers.

# Chapter 23
# Return to the Pleroma

The return to the Pleroma constitutes the consummation of the spiritual journey proposed by Esoteric Christianity and, at the same time, the restoration of a primordial condition that was lost but never extinguished. This trajectory is not a mere geographical ascent or a transposition of existential planes, but the reintegration of the soul to its original essence, unveiling its true identity as a direct emanation of the Supreme Source. From the moment the soul plunges into the experience of incarnation, enveloped by dense matter and the veils of ignorance, it carries within itself a silent longing for return, a subtle and incessant call that resonates in the deepest layers of consciousness. The Pleroma is not a distant place or a reality accessible only after death, but a dimension of fullness that pulsates in every soul, waiting to be recognized and experienced. Returning to the Pleroma, therefore, is less about moving from one point to another and more about removing the layers of illusion that prevent the direct perception of the divine light, which has never ceased to shine in the center of the human soul.

This process of return is made possible by the revelation of Gnosis, the sacred knowledge that not only informs but transforms. Gnosis reveals that the current condition of the soul, imprisoned in the material cosmos and subject to the designs of the Demiurge and his Archons, is an anomaly, a distortion of the original divine order. The true nature of the soul is not material, but spiritual; it is not a servant of the inferior creation, but an heir to the divine fullness. The Aeon Christ emerges as the one who, by crossing the veils of illusion and entering the world of matter, offers humanity not only a teaching, but a vibrational key capable of reactivating the forgotten spiritual memory. His role is to restore the lost bridge between the Pleroma and the fallen world, giving back to the soul the inner map that leads to its true home. The Aeonic Christ, by incarnating Gnosis itself, becomes not only the bearer of truth, but truth itself in living form, capable of resonating in the heart of the seeker and awakening in him the divine spark that echoes with the primordial light of the Pleroma.

Redemption, therefore, is a movement of reintegration and recognition. Each stage of the spiritual path — from inner purification to the unveiling of Gnosis, from the awakening of the divine spark to the transcendence of the conditioning imposed by the sensory world — is a preparation for this return. Liberation from the dominion of the Demiurge and his archontic forces does not occur through an external battle, but through the inner dissolution of identification with the ego, with the transient personality, and with the belief that matter is the only existing reality. As the soul awakens to its true divine nature, the shackles of the lower world lose their strength and the hidden portals to the Pleroma begin to open, not as an escape, but as a conscious reintegration into the higher cosmic order. This return to the Pleroma is the consummation of the work of the Aeonic Christ, the realization of the divine purpose of gathering all the scattered sparks into a single symphony of light and fullness, definitively dissolving the illusion of separation and restoring the original harmony between Creator and creation.

This return, however, does not nullify the individual experience of the soul, but elevates it to a new level of consciousness and existence. The soul is not dissolved in the Pleroma like a drop in the ocean, but rediscovers its true identity in communion with all other divine emanations. The limited individuality of the ego gives way to a full and divine individuation, where each soul recognizes its sacred uniqueness as a reflection of the Totality. The return to the Pleroma is, therefore, the consummation of a cosmic cycle, in which the fall into matter and spiritual exile are re-signified as part of a divine pedagogy, where the very experience of separation and forgetting serves as an impetus for an even more conscious and glorious return. The promise of redemption by the Aeon Christ is, ultimately, the promise that no soul is forgotten, no divine spark is lost, and that, through Gnosis and divine love, all emanations will return to the source from which they once departed, completing the great cycle of creation and cosmic reintegration.

The nature of the redemption offered by the Aeon Christ, from the Gnostic perspective, is fundamentally different from the traditional conceptions of orthodox Christianity. Gnostic redemption is not centered on the vicarious atonement of sins through the sacrifice of Christ on the cross, nor on salvation from eternal condemnation in a final judgment. Instead, redemption is understood as a process of spiritual liberation, an emancipation of the human soul from the prison of the material world and the dominion of the Demiurge, the imperfect creator of this cosmos. The human soul, in the Gnostic view, is essentially divine, a spark of light imprisoned in dense matter and obscured by ignorance. Redemption, therefore, implies the awakening of this divine spark, the recognition of one's true spiritual identity, and the breaking away from the illusion of the material world that keeps the soul captive.

The liberation from the material world, as a central aspect of Gnostic redemption, does not necessarily mean a physical escape or a denial of the body and earthly existence. Instead, liberation refers to a transformation of consciousness, a change of perspective that transcends the exclusive identification with material reality and opens up to the vastness of spiritual reality. The material world, in the Gnostic view, is seen as a realm of illusion, suffering, duality, and impermanence, created by an imperfect entity and governed by oppressive forces, the Archons, who seek to keep humanity in ignorance and captivity. Redemption, in this context, implies disentangling oneself from this illusion, breaking away from the conditioning of the material mind, and awakening to the spiritual truth that resides beyond the world of the senses.

The return to the Pleroma, the realm of divine fullness, represents the ultimate goal of Gnostic redemption and the final destiny of the liberated soul. The Pleroma, as the dwelling place of the Aeons and the Supreme Divinity, is the realm of light, truth, perfection, eternity, and joy. The human soul, in its divine essence, belongs to the Pleroma and longs for the return to this primordial home. Redemption, guided by the Aeon Christ and propelled by Gnosis, enables the soul to ascend from the lower spheres of material reality back to the Pleroma, reintegrating itself into the divine fullness and rediscovering the primordial unity with the Supreme Divinity. This return to the Pleroma is not merely a spatial or geographical movement, but an ontological transformation, a change in the soul's state of being, which transcends the limitation of individual existence and merges into the vastness and eternity of the divine realm.

The Aeon Christ, as the agent of redemption, plays a fundamental role in this process of liberation and return. He is the revealer of Gnosis, the guide on the spiritual path, and the very path to redemption. Christ's message, centered on Gnosis, offers the saving knowledge that dispels ignorance and frees the soul from illusion. His example of life and his teachings inspire and empower spiritual seekers to tread the journey of inner transformation, to break away from the conditioning of the material mind, and to awaken to their true divine nature. Christ not only teaches the path of redemption, but also intercedes for those who seek him, offering his help, his protection, and his divine grace to facilitate the journey of return to the Pleroma.

Redemption through the Aeon Christ, in the Gnostic perspective, is not a passive or automatic event, but an active and participatory process, which requires effort, dedication, and perseverance on the part of the spiritual seeker. Gnosis is not a free gift or a divine favor granted without effort, but the fruit of a sincere search, of a constant spiritual practice, and of an opening of the mind and heart to the divine truth. The Aeon Christ offers the necessary path and assistance, but the final responsibility for the journey of redemption lies with each individual. Gnostic redemption is, therefore, a cooperation between divine grace and human free will, between the redemptive action of the Aeon Christ and the personal effort of the spiritual seeker.

The promise of redemption through the Aeon Christ, with its emphasis on liberation from the material world and the return to the Pleroma, offers a vision of hope and radical transformation for exiled humanity. It invites us to transcend the limited and illusory view of earthly existence, to awaken to the spiritual truth that resides within the depths of being, and to tread the path of Gnosis in search of union with the Supreme Divinity. Gnostic redemption is not an escape from the world, but a transformation of consciousness in the world, an inner liberation that allows one to live earthly life with more fullness, awareness, and serenity, in the hope and certainty of the final return to the home of light. The message of redemption of the Aeon Christ resonates as a call to the spiritual journey, an invitation to the search for Gnosis, and a promise of liberation and fullness for all those who long for the return to the Pleroma and union with the divine.

# Chapter 24
# The Sacrifice of the Aeon Christ

The sacrifice of the Aeon Christ, from the perspective of esoteric Christianity, represents a cosmic surrender of dimensions incomprehensible to the ordinary mind, a voluntary renunciation of the luminous fullness of the Pleroma to penetrate the dense and fragmented layers of material existence. This immersion does not occur as an isolated act or as a response to a specific human error, but as a direct expression of divine love that continually seeks to restore the original unity. The Aeon Christ is not compelled to descend by an imposed duty or by a need to balance spiritual accounts, but by infinite compassion, moved by the deep desire to awaken the divine sparks imprisoned in the lower world and lead them back to the primordial source. His descent is the gesture of a divine being who, complete in himself, chooses to relinquish his transcendent glory to become accessible to the fragmented consciousness of fallen humanity, assuming the limitations of form and temporality to serve as a living bridge between the Pleroma and the lower creation.

This primordial sacrifice manifests itself on multiple levels. On the cosmic level, it signifies the self-exposure of the Aeonic Christ to the density of the sensible world, where the primordial harmony of the Pleroma gives way to duality, pain, and illusion. By entering this domain, the Aeon Christ not only touches matter, but allows himself to be enveloped by its limitations and assumes, by free choice, the vulnerability and impermanence inherent in incarnate existence. The very incarnation of the Aeonic Christ, therefore, is in itself a sacrifice, since it implies the temporary suspension of the direct experience of divine fullness, replaced by the condition of a being who walks among shadows, subject to the laws of the world created by the Demiurge and closely watched by the Archons, guardians of the gates of forbidden knowledge. Thus, the descent is, by its very nature, a cosmic crucifixion, where the pure spirit accepts being pierced by the chains of fragmentation and pain, not out of its own necessity, but to offer a way back to those who, without this intervention, would remain imprisoned in ignorance and the incessant cycle of material repetition.

On the historical and symbolic level, this sacrifice reaches its maximum expression in the crucifixion of Jesus, the incarnate manifestation of the Aeon Christ. More than a physical or political event, the crucifixion represents the archetypal enactment of the drama of the divine soul imprisoned in matter, the suffering inherent in luminous consciousness when confronted with the limitations and violence of the lower world. Each nail, each wound, and each instant of agony symbolizes the clash between light and darkness, between the memory of the Pleroma and the oppression of forgetting. However, this crucifixion is not a defeat, but a revelation. By accepting the cross, the Aeon Christ illuminates the very symbol of pain and death with the light of transcendence, transforming it into a portal for spiritual resurrection. It is not, in the Gnostic view, a vicarious atonement for individual sins, but the supreme demonstration that even in the heart of suffering, the divine spark remains alive and can be awakened, illuminating the path of return for all those who, inspired by this example, seek Gnosis.

This sacrifice, far from a passive offering, is a gesture of spiritual power. The Aeon Christ, by voluntarily descending into the world of form and forgetting, does not lose his connection with fullness, but carries with him the living memory of the Pleroma, anchoring it in human flesh and consciousness itself. He thus becomes the meeting point between the eternal and the transitory, between the invisible and the manifest. His sacrifice is the conscious offering of his own divine essence as a guiding thread so that each lost soul can follow this same path, awakening in itself the forgotten memory and rediscovering the hidden door of return. The sacrifice of the Aeon Christ is not just a remote event or exclusive to his person, but an archetypal model that is actualized in every seeker who, inspired by this surrender, decides to walk the path of Gnosis, sacrificing the illusions of the ego to rediscover, in himself, the eternal light that has never been extinguished.

The notion of "sacrifice" applied to the Aeon Christ differs significantly from the interpretation traditionally found in orthodox Christianity. In exoteric

Christianity, the sacrifice of Christ on the cross is central to the doctrine of vicarious atonement, where Jesus' death is seen as a sacrificial act that appeases divine wrath and pays the penalty for the sins of humanity. In esoteric Christianity, the emphasis shifts from the expiatory sacrifice to the descent of the Aeon Christ into the material world as the central event of redemption. The "descent" is interpreted as an act of divine condescension, motivated by love and compassion for humanity imprisoned in ignorance and suffering.

From this Aeonic perspective, Christ's "sacrifice" does not reside primarily in his physical death on the cross, but rather in the very act of abandoning the fullness of the Pleroma and penetrating the lower spheres of material reality. The descent of the Aeon Christ into the material world is, in itself, an act of self-limitation, a temporary renunciation of his divine glory and his dwelling in the uncreated light. Entering the realm of dense and illusory matter, submitting to the laws of the material world, and assuming a human form, albeit a manifested one, represent a "sacrifice" in the sense of voluntarily diminishing his full divine manifestation in order to become accessible to human perception and fulfill his redemptive mission.

Interpretations of Christ's suffering and crucifixion from the Aeonic perspective also take on a symbolic and esoteric character. Although the historicity of the crucifixion is not necessarily denied, the focus shifts from the literalness of physical suffering to its spiritual and archetypal meaning. Christ's suffering and crucifixion can be interpreted as allegories of the human condition, imprisoned in matter and subject to suffering, pain, and death. The cross, in this sense, is not only an instrument of torture, but a symbol of the duality inherent in material existence, of the conflict between spirit and matter, light and darkness, and of the suffering that arises from this duality.

Through the Aeonic lens, Christ's crucifixion can be seen as an act of identification with the suffering human condition, a voluntary immersion in the depths of pain and darkness to offer the light of Gnosis and the path of liberation. Christ, by experiencing suffering and crucifixion, would not be atoning for the sins of others in a legal sense, but rather experiencing the human condition itself in its fullness, in order to transform that condition from within and offer the hope of redemption. His suffering, therefore, is not an end in itself, but a means to achieve a greater purpose: the spiritual awakening of humanity and its liberation from the captivity of matter.

The meaning of Christ's descent as an act of love and redemption emerges as the key to understanding the Aeonic "sacrifice". The fundamental motivation for Christ's descent is not the atonement of human guilt or the satisfaction of a punitive divine justice, but rather the unconditional love of the Father for his exiled creation. The Aeon Christ is sent into the world as a manifestation of this divine love, as a messenger of hope and liberation, moved by compassion for suffering humanity. His "sacrifice" is, ultimately, an act of love, a voluntary surrender of himself for the good of humanity, a giving of his light and wisdom to dispel the darkness of ignorance and offer the path of return to the home of light.

The descent of the Aeon Christ, interpreted as an act of love and redemption, resonates with the very dynamics of divine emanation, where the Supreme Divinity manifests itself progressively in lower spheres of reality out of pure benevolence and abundance of being. Christ's "sacrifice," in this context, is not a loss or a diminution of divinity, but rather an expression of its overflowing fullness, an act of divine generosity that manifests itself for the good of creation. The Father's love, manifested in the descent of the Aeon Christ, is the redemptive force that permeates the Gnostic cosmos, the transforming energy that drives the soul's journey in search of Gnosis and the return to the Pleroma.

In short, the "sacrifice of the Aeon Christ" in the Gnostic perspective must be understood in a symbolic and esoteric way, far from the sacrificial and expiatory interpretations of exoteric Christianity. The true "sacrifice" lies in the voluntary descent of the Aeon Christ into the material world, an act of love and divine condescension motivated by compassion for humanity. Christ's suffering and crucifixion, symbolically reinterpreted, become allegories of the human condition and manifestations of the redemptive love of the Aeon Christ, who offers Gnosis as the path of liberation and return to divine fullness. The exploration of the "Sacrifice of the Aeon Christ" reveals the depth and nuance of Gnostic soteriology and its unique vision of redemption as a process of inner transformation driven by love and knowledge.

# Chapter 25
# Harmony and Cooperation in the Divine Realm

In the heart of the Pleroma, the divine fullness reveals itself as a vast network of luminous emanations, where each Aeon expresses a specific aspect of the intelligence and love of the Supreme Source. This superior spiritual reality is not fragmented or marked by tensions and disputes, but organized in a dynamic of perfect cooperation and spontaneous harmony, where each Aeon, without losing its identity and singular function, actively participates in the maintenance of cosmic balance and the expansion of divine light in all directions. This harmony does not arise from external rules or impositions, but from the very divine nature of each Aeon, which carries within itself the living memory of primordial unity and acts moved by an intrinsic desire to collaborate with others in the manifestation of the divine plan. The Pleroma is, therefore, a living organism of spiritual interrelationships, where the diversity of emanations does not break, but enriches the essential unity of divine light, reflecting the inexhaustible abundance of the Source itself.

In this context, the Aeon Christ occupies a position of utmost relevance, not as an isolated figure or holder of hierarchical privileges, but as the radiating center of the redeeming light that connects the higher spheres to humanity exiled in the material world. Christ is the link that synthesizes the fullness of the love and wisdom of the Pleroma and, through his descent, reveals and reestablishes the connection between human souls and the divine reality. However, this cosmic mission is not carried out independently or solitarily. Each stage of the divine emanation, from the first light emanated from the Source to the intermediate planes that support creation, counts on the active and loving participation of countless Aeons who, in total harmony, collaborate so that the light, wisdom, and vital energy of the Pleroma reach the lower regions, where human consciousness sleeps amidst illusion. The Aeon Christ, therefore, does not act as an isolated savior or divine hero, but as the focal point of a vast synergy of luminous emanations, whose constant cooperation ensures that redemption is a joint work, an expression of the solidarity and compassion of the divine totality.

This harmony and cooperation among the Aeons manifests itself in a particularly intense way in the redemptive mission. Each Aeon contributes directly or indirectly to the preparation of the path by which the human soul can return to its luminous origin. Sophia, for example, whose daring impulse gave rise to the creation of the material world and the fall of fragmented wisdom, is also the guardian of spiritual memory and the longing for return. She actively collaborates with the Aeon

Christ, inspiring the awakening of the human soul and whispering to restless hearts the call of the distant light. Likewise, the Holy Spirit, understood in the Gnostic tradition as a feminine emanation, acts as a life-giving breath, animating the soul during its journey through the veils of illusion and strengthening its longing for transcendence. Each Aeon, even if not directly visible or identified in historical and material processes, is an active participant in this redemptive symphony, offering their specific spiritual gifts to sustain the journey of return of human consciousness to the luminous bosom of the Pleroma.

This divine cooperation, however, is not restricted to the spiritual plane. It echoes as an archetypal model for awakened humanity, serving as an inspiration so that, even in the world fragmented by duality and conflict, it is possible to glimpse and build forms of coexistence based on harmony, cooperation, and the recognition of the sacredness of diversity. Just as the Aeons collaborate without competition or domination, each human soul, upon awakening to its true nature, is called to recognize in other seekers not rivals or threats, but spiritual allies in the great journey of return. The harmony of the Pleroma, reflected in the relationship between the Aeon Christ and the other Aeons, therefore, becomes a mirror of humanity's deepest vocation: to reconstitute, even in material exile, the living memory of lost communion, recreating in the plane of human experience the same symphony of love, cooperation, and unity that defines the divine realm.

The relationship of the Aeon Christ with other Aeons is primarily marked by harmony. Within the Pleroma, the absence of conflict or competition is an essential characteristic, reflecting the perfection and unity of the Supreme Divinity that manifests itself in fullness in this realm. The Aeons, as emanations of the same divine source, share a fundamentally luminous and benevolent nature, working together to sustain the cosmic order and radiate divine light to the lower spheres of reality. Harmony among the Aeons does not imply uniformity or absence of individuality, but rather a unity in diversity, where each Aeon, with its specific attributes and functions, contributes to the richness and complexity of the whole, without generating dissonance or imbalance.

The Aeon Christ, inserted in this harmonious community, relates to the other Aeons in a spirit of equality and mutual respect, recognizing the importance and uniqueness of each one within the divine plan. Although Christ's redemptive mission places him in a central role in Gnostic soteriology, he does not place himself above the other Aeons in terms of a hierarchy of power or ontological superiority. In the Pleroma, the Aeonic hierarchy is primarily functional, not hierarchical in the mundane sense of domination or subordination. Christ, in his relationship with the other Aeons, acts as a *primus inter pares*, a "first among equals," leading and guiding through love, wisdom, and inspiration, and not through imposition or arbitrary authority.

Cooperation among the Aeons is another fundamental principle that defines relationships within the Pleroma. The cosmic order and the realization of the divine plan are not the result of the isolated action of a single Aeon, but rather of the joint and coordinated action of the entire Aeonic community. Each Aeon performs specific functions, contributing its attributes and talents to the proper functioning of the whole. This cooperation is manifested in the organization of the cosmos, in the maintenance of divine order, in the irradiation of the light and wisdom of the Pleroma, and, crucially for humanity, in the mission of redemption and the pursuit of spiritual awakening.

The Aeon Christ, in his redemptive mission in the material world, does not act in isolation, but rather with the help and support of other Aeons. Sophia, the Divine Wisdom, plays a fundamental role in preparing the way for the coming of Christ and in restoring cosmic order after the fall. The Holy Spirit, a feminine Aeon, inspires, animates, and empowers spiritual seekers, guiding them on the path of Gnosis and strengthening their faith. Various other Aeons, with their specific qualities and attributes, contribute to Christ's mission, offering assistance, protection, and guidance to those who dedicate themselves to the search for spiritual truth. This interconnection of the Aeons demonstrates the unity of the Pleroma and the joint action of the divine community for the good of creation and for the redemption of humanity.

The harmony and cooperation among the Aeons for the organization of the cosmos reflect the intrinsic order of the Pleroma and the divine intelligence that permeates the spiritual realm. The Aeons act as organizing forces, maintaining cosmic balance, regulating natural cycles, and ensuring the harmony and stability of the spiritual and material universe. This cosmic organization is not rigid or mechanistic, but rather dynamic and fluid, reflecting the living and intelligent nature of the Pleroma. The joint action of the Aeons ensures that divine energy flows freely through the cosmos, sustaining life, consciousness, and evolution at all levels of reality.

In human redemption, the harmony and cooperation among the Aeons are manifested in a particularly relevant way. Gnosis, the salvific knowledge revealed by Christ, is not just a verbal message or a set of theoretical teachings, but rather a transformative force that acts in synergy with the energy of various Aeons to awaken human consciousness and lead the soul back to the Pleroma. The inspiration of the Holy Spirit, the wisdom of Sophia, the love of Christ, and the influence of other Aeons work together to propel the spiritual journey, offer assistance in times of difficulty, and guide the seeker of Gnosis towards union with the divine. This joint action demonstrates the solicitude and compassion of the Aeonic community for exiled humanity and its willingness to cooperate for the realization of redemption and the return to the home of light.

The exploration of the relationship of the Aeon Christ with other Aeons, emphasizing harmony and cooperation, reveals the beauty and depth of the Gnostic vision of the Pleroma as a realm of unity in diversity, of love and wisdom in action. Christ, inserted in this interconnected divine community, acts as a beacon of light and a compassionate guide, leading humanity back to the Pleroma with the help and support of all the Aeons. The understanding of harmony and cooperation in the divine realm inspires the search for unity and collaboration also in the human world, reflecting the Gnostic aspiration for a harmonious cosmos and for an awakened humanity united in the search for spiritual truth. The message of the Aeon Christ, in his relationship with the other Aeons, resonates as an invitation to communion, cooperation, and the pursuit of harmony at all levels of existence, reflecting the beauty and order of the divine realm in the heart of being.

# Chapter 26
# Personal Spiritual Practice

Personal spiritual practice based on conscious connection with the Aeons is founded on a deep understanding that authentic spirituality transcends the limits of intellect and doctrinal formulations, becoming a direct, sensitive, and transformative experience of divine reality. The Aeons, as emanations of the divine fullness and cosmic intelligences that express specific aspects of transcendent wisdom and love, manifest themselves not as distant or inaccessible abstractions, but as living presences that permeate the totality of being and the cosmos. The personal spiritual journey that seeks this connection starts from the awareness that each human being carries in their deepest core a spark of this same Aeonic reality, an inner reflection of the primordial wisdom that impels the soul in its quest for return to the divine. Thus, spiritual practice is not reduced to a set of external rituals, but represents a constant inner disposition to broaden perception, silence the illusions of the ego, and cultivate the spiritual sensitivity necessary to perceive and respond to the subtle presence of the Aeons in the flow of everyday existence.

The construction of this conscious connection involves the development of an inner state of receptivity and spiritual resonance, in which the mind, heart, and spirit harmonize in an attentive listening to the wisdom that emanates from the higher planes of reality. Each Aeon carries a specific vibration, a field of meaning and energy that expresses divine qualities such as love, truth, justice, beauty, compassion, and wisdom. Personal spiritual practice, therefore, consists of creating, within the being, a space of recognition and affinity with these qualities, allowing the presence of the Aeons to resonate and illuminate consciousness. This process does not occur instantaneously or mechanically, but requires patient cultivation, sincere surrender, and the willingness to traverse the layers of conditioning, limiting beliefs, and superficial identifications that obscure the direct perception of Aeonic reality. Each spiritual practice becomes, in this context, a living bridge between the manifest world and the divine fullness, between the incarnate soul and the transcendent wisdom that dwells in the heart of the Pleroma.

True personal spiritual practice focused on the Aeons is not content with the search for fleeting mystical experiences or isolated glimpses of the divine light, but is oriented towards a gradual and profound transformation of the very structure of consciousness and the way of being in the world. Connection with the Aeons is, at the same time, a revelation of the true nature of the soul and a call for this nature to be expressed in concrete existence, through actions, thoughts, and attitudes that reflect divine wisdom and love. Each conscious contact with the Aeons expands the understanding of the underlying unity between the human and the divine, dissolves the illusions of separateness, and awakens a sense of spiritual responsibility before creation. Thus, personal spiritual practice not only enriches the inner experience of Gnosis, but also transforms the seeker's relationship with the world, inviting them to be a living expression of Aeonic harmony in the fabric of existence. By cultivating this connection, the human being not only rediscovers their true place in the spiritual cosmos, but becomes a conscious collaborator in the unfolding of divine light amidst the shadows of matter, embodying the wisdom and love of the Aeons in every gesture, word, and intention of their spiritual journey.

Spiritual practices that aim to connect with the energy and wisdom of the Aeons can take various forms, adapting to the individuality and inclination of each seeker. The central point lies in the sincere intention to establish conscious communication with the Aeonic reality, opening oneself to its beneficial influence and seeking its guidance for the spiritual journey. These practices are not limited to formal rituals or religious dogmas, but rather to techniques and attitudes that cultivate interiorization, receptivity, and the opening of consciousness to the higher spiritual dimensions of reality.

Meditation emerges as a fundamental tool for connecting with the Aeons. Through meditative practice, the seeker can quiet the rational mind, silence the incessant flow of thoughts and everyday concerns, and create an inner space of receptivity and stillness conducive to the perception of Aeonic reality. Meditation directed towards the Aeons can involve visualizing their light and energy, invoking their names or attributes, contemplating their symbols and archetypes, or simply opening consciousness to their subtle and transformative presence. Regular and persistent meditation can generate a noticeable change in the perception of reality, making the seeker more receptive to divine inspirations, spiritual intuitions, and the beneficial influence of the Aeons.

Contemplation is another powerful spiritual practice for Aeonic connection. Unlike meditation, which seeks to quiet the mind, contemplation involves deep immersion in the nature of a specific Aeon, seeking to understand its attributes, its functions, and its role within Gnostic cosmology. Contemplation can be directed to a particular Aeon, such as Sophia, Christ, or the feminine Aeon Holy Spirit, seeking to absorb their wisdom, energy, and inspiration. Reading and reflecting on Gnostic texts that describe the Aeons can be a starting point for contemplation, aiding in intellectual understanding and paving the way for the intuitive and experiential experience of Aeonic reality. Contemplation can generate a profound transformation of consciousness, expanding the understanding of divine nature and strengthening the connection with the spiritual realm.

Beyond meditation and contemplation, other techniques can be used to establish a personal connection with the Aeons. Guided visualizations can help the mind to imagine the Pleroma, the abode of the Aeons, and to create a mental space for meeting and communicating with these cosmic intelligences. Prayer, when directed to the Aeons with sincerity and devotion, can open channels of spiritual communication and generate a flow of divine energy and inspiration. Artistic creation, such as painting, music, poetry, or dance, can be used as a way to express the experience of connection with the Aeons and to manifest their creative energy in the material world. Immersion in nature, contemplating the beauty and harmony of the natural world, can evoke the presence of the Aeons as organizing and animating forces of the cosmos, facilitating connection with their vital energy.

It is important to emphasize that the search for connection with the Aeons in personal spiritual practice should not be seen as a search for supernatural powers or selfish benefits. The main purpose is spiritual awakening, the transformation of consciousness, the pursuit of Gnosis, and union with the divine. Connection with the Aeons is a means to achieve this end, an aid in the soul's journey in search of truth and liberation. The fundamental attitude in Aeonic spiritual practice should be humility, receptivity, sincerity, and devotion, seeking connection with the Aeons with an open heart and with the intention of serving the divine plan and contributing to the common good.

The experience of connection with the Aeons in personal spiritual practice can be deeply transformative and enriching. It can generate a feeling of connection with something greater than limited individuality, a sense of purpose and direction in life, a source of inspiration and creativity, a strengthening of faith and hope, and a fuller experience of spirituality in everyday life. Aeonic spiritual practice can open the way for a deeper understanding of Gnostic cosmology, divine nature, and the soul's journey in search of Gnosis, leading to a richer and more meaningful experience of spiritual life.

In summary, personal spiritual practice that aims at connection with the Aeons offers a concrete and accessible path to experience the esoteric dimension of Christianity and to explore the richness of Gnostic cosmology. Through meditation, contemplation, and other techniques, the spiritual seeker can establish a conscious relationship with the energy and wisdom of the Aeons, enriching their journey of Gnosis and propelling their spiritual awakening. Aeonic spiritual practice invites a deep inner search, an opening to transcendent reality, and a fuller and more conscious experience of the divine presence in the heart of being and in the entire universe.

# Chapter 27
# Knowledge of the Aeons

The knowledge of the Aeons reveals itself as a process of direct access to the deepest and most authentic dimension of spiritual reality, where human consciousness aligns with the divine emanations that constitute the invisible fabric of the cosmos. In this context, the Aeons are not merely abstract entities or distant theological concepts, but living and dynamic expressions of divine thought itself, intermediaries between the Pleroma and the manifested world. Each Aeon carries within itself a portion of the divine mystery, bearing attributes, qualities, and powers that reflect specific aspects of eternal wisdom. To know the Aeons, therefore, implies tuning in to these spiritual powers, allowing their subtle vibrations to penetrate the soul and reveal the truth hidden behind appearances. This form of knowledge, however, transcends the simple accumulation of information or conceptual understanding; it is a lived integration, where the very identity of the seeker is transformed and elevated to the light of spiritual consciousness.

This process of connection with the Aeons occurs through the expansion of inner perception, a progressive opening of the mind and heart to the supra-rational dimensions of existence. Unlike ordinary knowledge, which is structured on linear logic and discursive analysis, the knowledge of the Aeons manifests as an intuitive, direct, and silent gnosis, in which truth is recognized not as something external to be acquired, but as a reality already present in the innermost core of being. Each stage of this path involves dissolving layers of conditioning, limiting beliefs, and illusory identifications that keep the soul imprisoned in the domain of time and matter. Only by removing these veils can consciousness rise to the luminous spheres where the Aeons dwell, receiving from them the keys to interpret one's own existence and the cosmic drama in which each human being participates.

The experience of direct contact with the Aeons does not represent a mystical escape from concrete reality, but rather a profound reintegration of the individual into the cosmic and divine totality. By knowing the Aeons, the seeker understands their true origin and destiny, perceiving themselves not as an isolated entity, subject to the vicissitudes of matter, but as a conscious spark within the eternal current of divine manifestation. This perception radically alters the way the world is viewed, as each event, each encounter, and each challenge comes to be seen as an opportunity to recognize and manifest the aeonic qualities latent within one's own being. The knowledge of the Aeons, therefore, is simultaneously an awakening of spiritual memory, an expansion of cosmic perception, and an ethical and existential transformation, leading to the reconciliation of the soul with its celestial origin and with the totality of the Pleroma.

Gnosis, as a direct experience of the knowledge of the Aeons and the divine realm, is radically distinguished from discursive and rational knowledge, proper to the material mind. Gnosis is not something that is learned in books or acquired through intellectual study, but rather something that is experienced in the core of being, a deep and transformative intuition of spiritual truth that transcends language and concepts. This direct experience of Gnosis is not a passive or fortuitous event, but rather the result of an active search, a constant spiritual practice, and an opening of consciousness to the transcendental dimensions of reality.

The path to Gnosis, as a direct experience of the Aeonic Realm, involves overcoming the illusion of the material world. Everyday perception, limited by the senses and the rational mind, presents a fragmented and superficial view of reality, obscuring the presence of the spiritual realm and imprisoning consciousness in the illusion of the material world. The search for Gnosis implies breaking with this illusion, freeing oneself from the conditioning of the material mind, and awakening to the deeper and truer reality that lies beyond the world of the senses. This overcoming of illusion does not mean denying material reality, but rather relativizing its importance and recognizing its transitory and imperfect nature in comparison with the eternity and fullness of the Aeonic Realm.

The search for Gnosis, as a path to transcend the illusion of the material world, manifests itself through various spiritual practices, such as meditation, contemplation, contemplative prayer, and deep introspection. These practices aim to quiet the rational mind, silence the internal dialogue, expand consciousness, and open a channel of direct communication with the higher spiritual dimensions of reality. Through persistent practice and sincere surrender, the seeker of Gnosis can access altered states of consciousness, experience mystical experiences, and intuit the presence of the Aeonic Realm within their being.

The accounts of Gnostic experiences throughout history testify to the reality of the direct experience of the Aeonic Realm and the profound transformation that Gnosis operates in the human soul. Gnostic texts, accounts of mystics, and testimonies of spiritual seekers describe experiences of visions of light, encounters with spiritual beings, states of ecstasy, sensations of unity with the cosmos, and intuitions of divine truth. These experiences, although varying in their form and content, share a common trait: the unmistakable feeling of connection with a reality deeper and truer than that which manifests itself to everyday perception, a reality that transcends the material world and resonates with the eternity and fullness of the Aeonic Realm.

The feeling of connection with the Aeons in the experience of Gnosis is not merely a subjective fantasy or a projection of the mind, but rather a real and objective perception of a dimension of reality that exists beyond the material world. The Aeons, as cosmic intelligences and divine forces, emit a subtle and powerful energy that can be perceived and experienced through the opening of consciousness and spiritual attunement. This connection with the Aeons can bring inspiration, wisdom, guidance, protection, and a deep sense of peace and joy. The experience of Gnosis as a connection with the Aeons strengthens the faith and hope of the spiritual seeker, confirming the reality of the divine realm and propelling their journey back to the Pleroma.

Gnosis, as a direct experience of the Aeonic Realm, is not an end in itself, but rather a path to transformation and spiritual liberation. The experience of Gnosis not only offers an intellectual knowledge of divine truth, but also operates a metamorphosis in the human soul, transforming its perception of reality, its values, its motivations, and its way of life. Gnosis awakens the inner divine spark, frees the soul from ignorance and illusion, and leads to union with the divine. The journey of Gnosis is not just a search for knowledge, but a search for integral transformation, a journey of self-knowledge, of purification of the mind and heart, and of opening to the fullness of spiritual life.

In summary, Gnosis, in esoteric Christianity, is understood as the direct experience of the Aeonic Realm, an intimate contact with the wisdom and light of the Aeons that transforms consciousness and leads to spiritual liberation. Achieving Gnosis through direct experience requires overcoming the illusion of the material world, constant spiritual practice, and the opening of consciousness to the transcendental dimensions of reality. The accounts of Gnostic experiences testify to the reality of this journey and the profound transformation that Gnosis operates in the human soul. The search for Gnosis as a direct experience of the Aeonic Realm represents the core of Gnostic spirituality, a path of self-knowledge, transformation, and union with the divine that resonates with the human thirst for transcendence and a deeper meaning in life.

# Chapter 28
# Guides on the Spiritual Path

The spiritual journey, from a Gnostic perspective, unfolds as a path of reconnection between the human soul and its divine origin. In this process, the presence of spiritual guides reveals itself not only as external assistance but as a direct expression of the divine wisdom that permeates all of creation. These guides, represented by the Aeons, do not appear as authoritarian masters who impose predetermined truths or paths, but as living emanations of the Pleroma, whose light and presence resonate within the human being, awakening their spiritual memory and strengthening their ability to discern inner truth. Each Aeon, with its specific qualities, acts as a key that unlocks dormant aspects of consciousness, offering not only knowledge but, above all, a vibration of love and silent guidance, which leads the soul beyond the limitations of the material world and the conditioning imposed by the archontic powers. The presence of the Aeons on the spiritual path is, therefore, both internal and external: they guide from within, as subtle voices of higher intuition, and from without, as inspirations and synchronicities that manifest in the course of existence, creating bridges between the visible and the invisible.

The action of the Aeons as spiritual guides is not restricted to specific moments of revelation or mystical ecstasy, but permeates the totality of the spiritual journey, from the first impulses of searching for meaning to the most elevated states of contemplation and spiritual union. Along this path, the soul learns to recognize the vibrational signature of each Aeon, discerning between the voices of the spirit and the noises of the ego or the archontic influences that seek to divert the seeker from their inner trajectory. The Aeons offer direct inspiration in the form of transformative insights, but they also instruct through challenges and trials that, when accepted with humility and discernment, serve to strengthen consciousness and deepen self-knowledge. This spiritual pedagogy, in which the very events of life become living and personalized lessons, reflects the organic nature of Aeonic wisdom, which does not separate learning and experience, but intertwines both in a single flow of growth and awakening.

The guiding presence of the Aeons reveals itself more intensely and clearly as the seeker cultivates inner openness and the ability to listen subtly, developing a spiritual sensitivity that transcends ordinary sensory perception. Meditation, contemplative prayer, stillness of mind, and sincere surrender to the divine flow create the conditions conducive to Aeonic guidance being perceived and integrated into daily life. However, this communication does not occur in discursive language or explicit commands; the Aeons speak through symbols, deep intuitions, and feelings of inner recognition, in which the truth reveals itself as a sudden remembrance of something that has always been present, but which had been covered by the fog of forgetfulness. Thus, following the guidance of the Aeons is, ultimately, a return to one's own spiritual center, where the divine presence already dwells as a constant whisper, awaiting only the soul's willingness to hear it and respond with confidence and devotion.

The Aeons, as guides and mentors in the individual spiritual journey, manifest themselves in various ways, adapting to the needs and receptivity of each seeker. They do not impose themselves or interfere with free will, but rather offer their assistance and guidance to those who sincerely seek truth and liberation. Their guidance is not dogmatic or authoritarian, but rather inspiring and persuasive, inviting the seeker to awaken their own intuition, discern the right path, and walk the spiritual journey with confidence and hope. The Aeons act as beacons of light, illuminating the path of Gnosis, removing obstacles, and offering the necessary support to overcome the challenges and difficulties inherent in the spiritual journey.

Seeking the inspiration of the Aeons on the spiritual path is to open oneself to the creative and luminous influence of the Pleroma. The Aeons, as emanations of the Supreme Divinity, radiate a spiritual energy that can inspire, motivate, and energize the seeker of Gnosis. This inspiration can manifest as intuitive insights, sudden understandings, creative ideas, feelings of enthusiasm and inner strength, boosting spiritual practice and fueling the search for truth. The inspiration of the Aeons is not just a fleeting sensation, but a transformative force that can direct the life and action of the seeker, guiding them towards the fulfillment of their spiritual purpose and the realization of their divine potential. Openness to Aeonic inspiration can be cultivated through meditation, contemplation, prayer, and conscious receptivity to the spiritual presence in all aspects of life.

In addition to inspiration, the Aeons offer protection on the spiritual path, supporting the seeker of Gnosis against negative influences and dangers that may arise on the journey. The material world, in the Gnostic view, is a realm of illusion and suffering, governed by hostile forces, the Archons, who seek to keep humanity in ignorance and spiritual captivity. The Aeons, as forces of light and power, act as protectors against these negative influences, creating a spiritual force field that supports and defends the seeker of Gnosis. This protection is not magical or superstitious, but rather the result of conscious connection with Aeonic energy, which strengthens the spirit, dispels the darkness of ignorance, and wards off harmful influences that can divert the seeker from the path of truth. Seeking the protection of the Aeons involves faith, devotion, prayer, and the sincere intention to follow the path of Gnosis under their guidance and protection.

The wisdom of the Aeons is an invaluable treasure for the spiritual seeker. The Aeons, as cosmic intelligences and divine archetypes, possess a profound knowledge of the nature of reality, the path of redemption, and the divine plan for humanity. This wisdom can be accessed through contemplation, meditation, reading Gnostic texts, and receptivity to intuition. The wisdom of the Aeons is not limited to factual information or theoretical doctrines, but rather to transformative insights, deep understandings, and practical guidance that help the seeker to discern the right path, make wise decisions, overcome life's challenges, and advance on the spiritual journey with discernment and clarity. Seeking the wisdom of the Aeons is to cultivate humility, open-mindedness, and receptivity to the voice of intuition and to the divine guidance that manifests through the Aeonic community.

The personal and devotional relationship with the Aeons as sources of spiritual assistance deeply enriches the journey of Gnosis. Although esoteric Christianity does not emphasize personal devotion to the same degree as exoteric Christianity, the recognition of the presence and influence of the Aeons as spiritual guides can generate a feeling of gratitude, reverence, and connection with the divine community. This personal relationship is not limited to formal rituals or repetitive prayers, but rather to an inner attitude of openness, receptivity, and trust in the guidance and protection of the Aeons. Cultivating this personal relationship can strengthen the faith, hope, and perseverance of the spiritual seeker, making the journey of Gnosis more meaningful, inspiring, and rewarding.

Seeking the inspiration, protection, and wisdom of the Aeons on the spiritual path does not imply delegating responsibility for one's own journey or passively depending on divine intervention. The journey of Gnosis remains a personal and active undertaking, which requires effort, discernment, and free will. The Aeons offer their assistance and guidance, but the decision to follow the path of Gnosis and to walk the spiritual journey with perseverance and dedication remains an individual choice. The Aeons act as facilitators and catalysts of the spiritual journey, but the inner transformation and the realization of Gnosis depend, ultimately, on the response and action of the seeker.

In short, the Aeons emerge as precious guides and loving mentors on the Gnostic spiritual path, offering inspiration, protection, and wisdom to those who seek Gnosis and union with the divine. Seeking their guidance and assistance through personal spiritual practice profoundly enriches the soul's journey, strengthening faith, hope, and perseverance, and propelling the seeker towards the realization of their spiritual potential and the encounter with divine truth. The personal and devotional relationship with the Aeons as sources of spiritual assistance reveals the beauty and depth of the Gnostic vision of the divine community and its loving care for humanity in search of redemption.

# Chapter 29
# The Awakening to Divine Reality

The awakening to divine reality consists of a profound reversal of perception, in which human consciousness, slumbering under the dense layers of material illusion, gradually turns towards the original light of its spiritual essence. This awakening process does not occur instantaneously or arbitrarily, but results from a delicate and constant interaction between the individual soul and the divine emanations that permeate the cosmos—the Aeons. These luminous beings, which represent the eternal attributes and intelligences of the Pleroma, radiate a subtle and incessant presence, whose primary function is to serve as a bridge between the fragmented consciousness of humanity and the indivisible fullness of spiritual reality. Every impulse of questioning, every intuition of a vaster truth, and every feeling of inadequacy in the face of the limited answers of the material world are signs that the Aeons are already touching the soul, stimulating it to seek what transcends appearances and to remember its divine origin. This awakening, therefore, is not just a discovery of new knowledge, but the recovery of an ancestral spiritual memory, a vibrant recollection of who we truly are on the eternal plane.

The action of the Aeons in the awakening of consciousness is not coercive or invasive; it is a loving and patient influence, adjusted to the rhythm and receptivity of each soul. The Aeons respect the freedom of the seeker and never impose truths or paths, but offer signs, inspirations, and silent invitations that awaken the divine spark within and lead consciousness beyond the narrow boundaries of ordinary perception. Their messages can arrive in the form of symbolic dreams, meaningful coincidences, sudden premonitions, or moments of spiritual clarity in the midst of common routine. Each manifestation of this subtle guidance is intended to destabilize the mind's fixation on superficial reality and stimulate the search for a deeper understanding of existence. This inner calling, provoked by the Aeons, ignites the longing for truth and inaugurates the process of disidentification with the limits of personality and matter, leading the soul to the vibrational field of Gnosis, where truth is not learned as external data, but recognized as something that has always existed within.

True awakening, therefore, does not consist only in seeing new realities or accessing higher planes of existence, but in completely transforming the very structure of the soul's perception. It is a mutation of consciousness itself, which ceases to perceive itself as an isolated and separate center and begins to recognize itself as a direct emanation of the divine source, destined to return to its origin through the experiential and direct knowledge of truth. This mutation is facilitated by intentional openness to the influence of the Aeons, by the practice of inner contemplation, and by the cultivation of a silent listening to the subtle voice of spiritual intuition. As consciousness awakens, external reality is also transfigured: the world, previously perceived as a disconnected set of objects and events, begins to be seen as a living tapestry of symbols and reflections of the divine, in which every instant and every encounter become opportunities to deepen communion with the sacred. The journey of Gnosis, thus, reveals itself as a progressive fusion between the inner gaze and the light of the Aeons, culminating in the full integration between individual consciousness and the vastness of Divine Reality.

The role of the Aeons in the transformation of human consciousness manifests itself on various levels and dimensions, encompassing both the individual and collective planes. The Aeons, as cosmic forces and divine intelligences, radiate a transformative energy that permeates the cosmos and subtly influences human consciousness, awakening the longing for truth, the search for Gnosis, and the aspiration for union with the divine. This influence is not imposing or deterministic, but rather inspiring and catalytic, offering opportunities for awakening and transformation to those who show themselves receptive and open to their influence.

The awakening of consciousness to divine reality is a gradual and progressive process, which begins with the recognition of the illusion of the material world and the limited nature of everyday perception. Human consciousness, conditioned by corporeality, the rational mind, and the influences of the material world, is asleep, identified with the transient and illusory reality, and forgetful of its true spiritual nature and its divine origin. The awakening of consciousness implies breaking with this illusory identification, detaching oneself from the conditioning of the material mind, and opening oneself to the intuition of the deeper and truer reality that lies beyond the world of the senses.

The Aeons, through their energy and influence, act as awakeners of consciousness, stimulating existential questioning, the longing for transcendence, and the search for a deeper meaning in life. Their subtle presence in the human psyche can manifest as intuitive insights, premonitions, synchronicities, meaningful dreams, and mystical experiences that challenge the conventional worldview and point to the existence of a spiritual reality underlying material reality. These "signs" of the awakening of consciousness can be subtle and easily ignored by the distracted mind, but when recognized and welcomed, they can initiate a process of questioning, searching, and inner transformation.

The search for the transformation of consciousness as part of the Gnostic path involves the practice of various techniques and attitudes that aim to expand perception, quiet the rational mind, and open oneself to the experience of Gnosis. Meditation, contemplation, contemplative prayer, the study of Gnostic texts, and introspective reflection are valuable tools for cultivating attentive awareness, spiritual discernment, and receptivity to the influence of the Aeons. These practices are not mere mental exercises or relaxation techniques, but rather methods of inner transformation, which aim to purify the mind and heart, expand the perception of reality, and open a channel of conscious communication with the higher spiritual dimensions.

The transformation of consciousness, driven by the influence of the Aeons and cultivated through spiritual practice, leads to a radical change in the perception of reality. The seeker of Gnosis, as he awakens to divine reality, begins to perceive the material world with new eyes, discerning its transient and illusory nature, and glimpsing the presence of divine light and spiritual energy in all things. This new perception of reality does not imply an escape from the world or a disregard for earthly life, but rather a more conscious and full experience of the present, a relativization of the importance of material concerns, and a valuing of the spiritual dimension of existence.

The awakening of consciousness to divine reality, driven by the Aeons and cultivated by the practice of Gnosis, is not just an altered state of perception, but rather an integral transformation of the being. Gnosis is not limited to intellectual knowledge or a momentary experience, but rather a continuous process of metamorphosis, which encompasses the mind, heart, will, and action of the spiritual seeker. The transformation of consciousness manifests itself in changes in behavior, new values, more authentic relationships, greater compassion, more serenity, and a fuller experience of love and joy. This integral transformation of being is the mark of true Gnosis, the sign of spiritual awakening, and the proof of the transformative action of the Aeons in human consciousness.

In summary, the Aeons play a fundamental role in the transformation of human consciousness, acting as agents of awakening and catalysts of metamorphosis towards Divine Reality. The awakening of consciousness, driven by the influence of the Aeons and cultivated through the practice of Gnosis, leads to a radical change in the perception of reality, an integral transformation of being, and a fuller and more conscious experience of spirituality in everyday life. The journey of Gnosis, in its essence, is a search for the transformation of consciousness, a path of awakening to spiritual truth and the realization of the divine potential inherent in every human being, guided and supported by the loving and transformative presence of the Aeons.

# Chapter 30
# Aeons in Contemporary Spirituality

The conceptual and spiritual presence of the Aeons resurfaces in the contemporary scene as a vibrant response to the profound anxieties of a humanity that, amidst the collapse of traditional belief structures, rediscovers in inner spirituality a legitimate path to meaning and reconnection with the divine. The Aeons, understood as living emanations of divine fullness and cosmic intelligences that mediate between the Pleroma and manifestation, offer a symbolic and experiential map for the modern soul seeking guidance amidst the excess of superficial information and the fragmented spiritual offerings of the digital age. This rediscovery is not mere esoteric nostalgia, but an authentic resonance between Gnostic cosmology and the contemporary thirst for experiential transcendence, for a spirituality that unites mystical intuition, profound self-knowledge, and cosmic understanding of existence. In this revival, the Aeons cease to be merely mythological figures of an ancient religious system and become real spiritual allies, subtle presences that echo in the collective psyche and in the ancestral memory of the human soul, summoning it to a journey of reintegration and awakening.

The growing fascination with Aeons in contemporary spirituality also stems from their symbolic plasticity, which allows for multiple readings and appropriations without diluting their profound essence. While in classical Gnostic traditions the Aeons were understood as celestial hierarchies structured in successive emanations, today they can be seen as dynamic archetypes of the psyche, formative forces of consciousness, or even as specific vibrational frequencies that permeate the fabric of the universe. This interpretive flexibility makes the Aeons particularly attractive to spiritual seekers who navigate between traditions, combining elements of esoteric Christian mysticism, Hermeticism, Jungian psychology, and spiritual practices of Eastern origin. At the same time, the notion that the Aeons are not just ideas or symbols, but real, intelligent, and compassionate presences that actively participate in the transformation of human consciousness, gives the concept a powerful experiential dimension, capable of nourishing both contemplative practices and therapeutic processes of self-knowledge and individuation.

In contemporary spiritual practice, interaction with the Aeons takes on personal and adaptable contours, reflecting the current emphasis on spiritual autonomy and the direct dialogue between the soul and higher forces, without institutional intermediaries. Each seeker, upon awakening to the existence of these cosmic intelligences, is invited to develop their own relationship of recognition, listening, and dialogue with the Aeons, whether through silent meditation, symbolic contemplation, or direct invocation of these presences. This openness to a relational spirituality, in which the divine is not a distant and inaccessible entity, but a living community of luminous consciousnesses in constant communication with the soul, transforms the spiritual quest into a journey of reunion, remembrance, and creative cooperation. Thus, the Aeons, recovered from Gnostic cosmology, emerge as spiritual beacons of a new era, guiding a fragmented humanity back to essential unity, not by dogmatic imposition, but by the loving invitation to inner awakening and conscious participation in the eternal dance of Creation.

The relevance of the concept of Aeons for contemporary spirituality lies in its ability to respond to various needs and yearnings of the human soul in modern times. In a context marked by religious pluralism and the crisis of traditional institutions, the concept of Aeons offers an inclusive and non-dogmatic view of spiritual reality, which transcends conventional religious boundaries and resonates with the spiritual experience of various cultures and traditions. The notion of a hierarchy of spiritual beings, intermediaries between the Supreme Deity and the material world, finds parallels in various spiritual currents, from Neoplatonism and Hermeticism to Buddhism and Hinduism, facilitating interreligious dialogue and the search for common ground in the experience of faith.

In an increasingly secularized and rationalistic world, the concept of Aeons offers a rich and profound symbolic and metaphorical language to express the mystical and transcendent dimension of reality, without resorting to rigid dogmas or literal and fundamentalist interpretations. The idea of Aeons as divine archetypes, organizing forces of the cosmos, and manifestations of the Supreme Deity resonates with contemporary sensibility, which values personal experience, intuition, and the search for a deeper meaning beyond instrumental reason and reductionist materialism. The concept of Aeons offers a spiritual vocabulary that allows exploring the complexity of divine reality and the richness of mystical experience in an open, creative, and personally meaningful way.

In an age of searching for meaning and purpose amidst chaos and uncertainty, the concept of Aeons offers a comprehensive and hopeful cosmological vision, which situates human existence in a vast and meaningful cosmic context. Gnostic cosmology, with its Aeonic hierarchy and its vision of the Pleroma as a realm of light and fullness, offers a spiritual map for the soul's journey, indicating the path of redemption, transformation, and return to the divine origin. The understanding of the Aeons as spiritual guides and mentors offers comfort, hope, and direction in times of crisis and uncertainty, strengthening faith and perseverance in the search for truth and the realization of spiritual potential.

The understanding of the Aeons can enrich the modern spiritual quest in several ways. First, the concept of Aeons offers an alternative to the anthropomorphic and personalistic view of God, present in many religious traditions, allowing the exploration of divine nature as something vaster, more mysterious, and transcendent, which manifests itself in multiple forms and intelligences. This broader and more inclusive view of divinity may resonate with those who feel disconnected from traditional images of God and who seek a more cosmic spirituality less centered on dogmas and formal rituals.

Second, the concept of Aeons values mystical experience and intuitive knowledge as pathways to spiritual reality, as opposed to the exclusive emphasis on dogmatic faith and religious authority. Gnosis, as direct experience of the Aeonic Realm, becomes the privileged path to understanding divine truth and transforming consciousness, encouraging inner searching, meditation, contemplation, and openness to spiritual intuition. This emphasis on direct experience and self-knowledge resonates with the contemporary search for a more authentic, personal, and transformative spirituality.

Third, the concept of Aeons offers a rich and symbolic vocabulary to explore the complexity of the human psyche and the dynamics of the spiritual journey. The Aeons, as divine archetypes, can be understood as symbolic images of deep psychic forces and processes that operate in the collective unconscious and shape human experience. The exploration of the Aeons as archetypes can enrich self-knowledge, the understanding of human nature, and the journey of individuation, offering a symbolic map for exploring the depths of the soul.

The enduring legacy of Gnostic and Aeonic thought in the world today lies in its ability to offer an alternative, inclusive, experiential, and transformative spirituality that resonates with the deep yearnings of the human soul in contemporary times. The concept of Aeons, rescued from historical oblivion, emerges as a precious jewel from the treasure of ancestral wisdom, offering an enriching path for the modern spiritual quest, the understanding of divine nature, and the realization of the human potential for transcendence and union with the divine. The relevance of the Aeons in contemporary spirituality is not merely theoretical or intellectual, but practical and existential, offering an enduring legacy that can inspire, guide, and transform the lives of those who open themselves to its wisdom and its call to the pursuit of Gnosis. In a world in constant change and transformation, the message of the Aeons remains as a beacon of hope and an invitation to the spiritual journey, echoing through the centuries and resonating with the human thirst for meaning, truth, and transcendence.

# Chapter 31
# The Human Evolution and Esoteric Christianity

The evolution of humanity, from the perspective of esoteric Christianity, is understood as a cosmic movement integrated into a broader flow of return to the divine origin, in which each soul, as a spark of the primordial light, is called to consciously participate in the restoration of lost unity. This process is not restricted to the technical, social, or even intellectual development of the species, but involves an essential transformation of human consciousness, capable of expanding its limited perception of reality and integrating it into the spiritual order that sustains creation. Humanity, throughout its historical trajectory, is invited to gradually awaken to the remembrance of its true nature, breaking free from the shackles of material illusion and the archontic control systems that obscure spiritual vision. The Aeons, in this context, do not figure only as distant archetypes or mythological symbols of an ancient cosmology, but as active intelligences and collaborators in the very evolution of collective consciousness, playing the role of divine catalysts that help humanity to traverse its phases of forgetfulness, crisis, and spiritual renewal.

Within this evolutionary panorama, the function of the Aeons transcends that of mere mediators between divinity and the material world. They constitute a true matrix of spiritual potentialities that permeate human consciousness at all levels, from the most primordial archetypal impulses to the most elevated inspirations that guide the soul in its search for truth. Each Aeon represents a facet of divine intelligence that manifests itself in the evolutionary process, offering humanity fragments of the memory of the Pleroma so that, through experience, inner searching, and spiritual practice, these luminous seeds can germinate and blossom into experiential wisdom. This intertwining between human spiritual evolution and the continuous emanation of Aeonic light allows us to understand the history of humanity not as a fortuitous chain of material events, but as a symbolic journey of learning and reintegration, where each challenge, each rupture, and each illumination represents an opportunity for renewed contact with the transcendent flow of the Pleroma.

Thus, esoteric Christianity, by rescuing the centrality of Gnosis and the living relationship with the Aeons, offers an evolutionary vision that unfolds on multiple levels: personal, collective, and cosmic. On the personal level, each soul is called to remember its divine origin, recognizing the Aeons as living presences that guide its journey of self-knowledge, liberation, and return. On the collective level, humanity as a spiritual organism moves towards overcoming the materialistic and fragmented paradigm that dominates its perception, being gradually led to the restoration of an integrating spirituality that rescues the sacredness of life and existence as an expression of divine light. And, on a cosmic scale, this human evolution participates in a larger movement of reconciliation between the worlds, where the very drama of separation between spirit and matter is progressively dissolved as consciousness awakens to the essential unity between the visible and the invisible. In this way, human history, illuminated by the light of the Aeons and guided by the call of Gnosis, reveals itself as an ascending spiral of conscious return to divine fullness, where the very evolution of humanity becomes a living sacrament of cosmic reintegration.

Throughout this work, we began our exploration by defining and delimiting esoteric Christianity, differentiating it from exoteric Christianity and highlighting its relevance in the current religious scene. We delved into the primary sources for understanding the Aeons, the Apocryphal Gospels and the Nag Hammadi texts, unveiling the richness and uniqueness of these writings that reveal an esoteric perspective of the Christian message. We entered into Gnostic cosmology, understanding the universe as a complex field of divine forces, emanating from the Supreme Divinity (Monad) and manifested through the hierarchy of the Aeons, organizing forces and cosmic intelligences that inhabit the Pleroma, the divine fullness.

We explored in depth the nature and hierarchy of the Aeons, unveiling the process of emanation from the Pleroma, the hierarchical structure and the Aeonic families, such as the singular importance of the Aeon Sophia and her cosmic fall. We dedicated special attention to the figure of Christ as the Savior Aeon, understanding his role as a revealer of Gnosis and a guide to redemption, and analyzing his position in the Aeonic hierarchy and the specificity of his mission in the material world. We also explored the Holy Spirit as a feminine Aeon, highlighting her function as the divine force of life and inspiration. We discerned the relationship between the Aeons and the creation of the material world by the Demiurge, understanding the Gnostic view of the origin of the cosmos and the duality between spirit and matter.

We investigated the functions of the Aeons, understanding their role in cosmic organization, human evolution, and redemption. We explored the relationship between the Aeons and time, contrasting Aeonic eternity with human linear perception. We analyzed the Aeonic variations in different Gnostic systems, comparing the hierarchies and names in various schools of thought. We reflected on the historical criticisms of the concept of Aeons and the modern interpretations in philosophy, psychology, and contemporary spirituality, seeking to evaluate the relevance of the study of the Aeons in the 21st century.

We deepened the analysis of Christ in the Aeonic context, exploring his divine nature and redemptive mission, his place in the hierarchy, his mission in the material world as a revealer of Gnosis, and the message of love and knowledge present in the Gospel of Truth and the secret teachings of the Gospel of Thomas. We differentiated the Aeonic Christ from the Historical Jesus, seeking to integrate both perspectives for a deeper understanding of the esoteric Christian message. We discussed the intrinsic relationship between the Aeon Christ and Gnosis, understanding saving knowledge as the path to redemption and return to the Pleroma. We explored the concept of redemption by the Aeon Christ, understanding it as liberation from the material world and return to divine fullness. We discussed the idea of a "sacrifice" of the Aeon Christ, reinterpreting it symbolically as the descent into the material world to save humanity. We analyzed the relationship of the Aeon Christ with other Aeons, emphasizing harmony and cooperation in the divine realm.

In the final part of our exploration, we connected the Aeons to human experience and the individual spiritual quest. We suggested spiritual practices to connect with the energy and wisdom of the Aeons, such as meditation and contemplation. We explored Gnosis as a direct experience of the Aeonic Realm, seeking to achieve knowledge of the Aeons through personal experience. We understood the Aeons as guides on the spiritual path, offering inspiration, protection, and wisdom. We analyzed the role of the Aeons in the transformation of consciousness, driving the awakening to the Divine Reality. Finally, we reflected on the relevance of the Aeons in contemporary spirituality, highlighting the enduring legacy of Gnostic and Aeonic thought in the modern world.

In final reflection, the understanding of the Aeons, rescued from esoteric Christianity, offers a rich and inspiring legacy for human spirituality. It invites us to rediscover the mystical and symbolic dimension of reality, to recognize the existence of broader and deeper planes of consciousness, and to seek a more direct and meaningful connection with the divine. The concept of Aeons, with its complex cosmology and its differentiated soteriology, enriches our understanding of Christianity, unveiling esoteric and mystical dimensions that transcend the exoteric and dogmatic view. Beyond the specific religious context, the study of the Aeons resonates with deep longings of the human soul, the search for meaning, the thirst for transcendence, and the aspiration for union with the ultimate mystery of existence.

The final message that emerges from this journey is the importance of the search for Gnosis and connection with the divine realm as an essential path for human evolution. In a world marked by materialism, rationalism, and fragmentation, Gnosis offers a path of wholeness, inner transformation, and reconnection with our own divine essence. The understanding of the Aeons, as guides and auxiliary forces in this journey, offers hope, inspiration, and direction for those who dedicate themselves to the search for spiritual truth and the realization of their highest human potential. May this exploration of the Esoteric Interpretations of Christianity and the Aeons inspire the reader to tread the path of Gnosis, to awaken to divine reality, and to experience the fullness of spiritual life, in search of union with the ultimate mystery of existence and the conscious evolution of the human soul.

# Epilogue

There are books that conclude on their final pages, and there are those that, upon completion, open portals. This is one of the latter. The journey you have undertaken throughout these pages was not a mere intellectual crossing, nor a succession of distant concepts, detached in time or space. Each word and each revelation echoed in deep layers of your consciousness, summoning forgotten fragments of your own spiritual history. Because, more than conveying information, this book aimed to remind. And to remind is to awaken.

The Aeons, those spiritual powers that sustain the fabric of the universe, are not just mythological characters or philosophical abstractions. They are living marks of cosmic memory, pulsating in every soul that dares to look within and listen to the ancestral call that resonates in their own spiritual blood. They were here before the first words, before the first religions, even before man knew himself as human. They were hidden, demonized, fragmented, and relegated to the shadows of apocryphal texts and hermetic traditions, but they never disappeared. They cannot disappear because they are part of the very fabric of existence—and part of you.

This path you have traveled was not just a visit to a lost esoteric Christianity. It was a return to the roots of something greater than any dogma or belief system. Because the Aeons, these emanations of divine fullness, are not external figures. They are mirrors of what dwells in the core of your soul: ordering principles, living fields of intelligence and love, spiritual guides that echo in your deepest intuitions, in your quietest anxieties, and in your sudden understandings that seem to come from nowhere. This book, in essence, merely revealed what you always knew, but were taught to forget.

The understanding of Aeonic cosmology is not an end, but an invitation to a new way of perceiving reality. The universe that once seemed fragmented between the visible and the invisible, the spiritual and the material, the divine and the human, now reveals itself as a single living current, flowing from the Primordial Source, through the Aeons, and reaching you. Your existence, your thoughts, your choices, and your experiences are not disconnected from this great spiritual body. You are an active part of this flow—a spark of the Pleroma temporarily immersed in the veil of matter. But this veil is not absolute. It is thin. And you have just torn it.

The Aeons, whose names resonate like forgotten echoes in ancient texts, are no longer distant figures, isolated in invisible layers of the sky. They reveal themselves as internal presences, living aspects of your own higher soul, guides that reflect and amplify the wisdom that, from the beginning, has inhabited your innermost being. Knowing that they exist is only the first step. Recognizing them in your own inner movements is the true awakening. And, even more, it is to realize that every search, every spiritual anguish, every yearning for something greater is, in fact, the echo of their call—a summons to reintegration.

If dogma stifled this truth, it was only out of fear of its transformative power. A soul that recognizes its direct connection with divine intelligence cannot be imprisoned by external formulas. A soul that understands that its redemption does not depend on mediators, but on its own inner alignment with the luminous flow of the Aeons, is not manipulable. This liberating truth was erased from official texts, but preserved in silence by esoteric currents that, century after century, guarded this invisible flame until there were souls ready to remember it.

Now, this flame has been placed in your hands. What will you do with it? Close this book and return to the comfort of superficial certainties, or move forward, exploring the sacred territories of your own being? Because true knowledge—Gnosis—does not reside in theories or beliefs. It pulsates in the heart of direct experience, in the dissolution of the boundaries between what you consider divine and what you consider human. The Aeons are not external entities that you should venerate. They are internal principles that you must awaken.

The return to the Pleroma—this luminous field of divine fullness—is not a distant destination. It is an intimate reconnection. It is not about a place outside of you, but about a reality hidden by layers of limiting beliefs and self-forgetfulness. Every sincere meditation, every deep contemplation, every true questioning dissolves a little of this illusory separation. Every time you recognize in yourself an echo of the primordial light, you take a step towards this reintegration.

Remember: your soul was not born in time. It is prior to it. It was cast into matter by a cosmic unfolding, but its essence remains intact, in eternal resonance with the spiritual forces that sustain the cosmos. You are not just an isolated individual—you are a conscious cell of the divine body itself. Every learning, every awakening, every recognition of this connection is an expansion of the universe itself, which only fully exists when its parts recognize themselves as part of the whole.

What has been offered here is not a closed system of beliefs. It is a reminder. A lost password. A subtle code inscribed in the deep layers of the human soul, waiting for the right moment to be read and deciphered. This moment has arrived for you.

The journey, however, does not end here. No book can contain the totality of the divine experience. No doctrine can imprison the constant movement of revelation. What you have received is only a lit torch. The path ahead—inner and cosmic—depends on what you will do with this light.

Allow yourself to continue. Allow yourself to deconstruct and reconstruct your certainties. Allow yourself to be guided not by external authorities, but by the silent intuitions that flow from your own connection with the Aeons. Because truth cannot be given—it can only be remembered.

And now, it resonates within you.
Sincerely,
Luiz Santos Editor

www.ingramcontent.com/pod-product-compliance
Lightning Source LLC
LaVergne TN
LVHW041924070526
838199LV00051BA/2710